The Family
and
Pastoral Care

HERBERT ANDERSON

The Family and Pastoral Care

Don S. Browning, *editor*

THEOLOGY AND PASTORAL CARE

FORTRESS PRESS
PHILADELPHIA

COPYRIGHT © 1984 BY FORTRESS PRESS

Library of Congress Cataloging in Publication Data
Anderson, Herbert, 1936–
  The family and pastoral care.
  (Theology and pastoral care series)
  1. Church work with families. 2. Family—Religious
life. 3. Family psychotherapy. I. Title. II. Series.
BV4438.A53 1984   253.5   83–48914
ISBN 0–8006–1728–2

K462L83   Printed in the United States of America   1–1728

Contents

68728

Series Foreword

Our purpose in the Theology and Pastoral Care Series is to present
ministers and church leaders with a series of readable books that will
(1) retrieve the theological and ethical foundations of the Judeo-
Christian tradition for pastoral care, (2) develop lines of communication between pastoral theology and the other disciplines of theology, (3) create an ecumenical dialog on pastoral care, and (4) do this
in such a way as to affirm, yet go beyond, the recent preoccupation of
pastoral care with secular psychotherapy and the other social sciences.

The books in this series are written by authors who are well
acquainted with psychology, psychotherapy, and the other social
sciences. All of the authors affirm the importance of these disciplines
for modern societies and for ministry in particular, but they see
them also as potentially destructive of human values unless they are
guided in their practical application by tested religious and ethical
traditions. But to retrieve the best of the Judeo-Christian tradition
for the church's care and counseling is a challenging intellectual
task—a task to which few writers in the area of pastoral care have
attended with sufficient thoroughness. This series addresses that
task out of a broad ecumenical stance, with all of the authors taking
an ecumenical approach to theology. Besides a vigorous investiga-
tion of Protestant resources, there are specific treatments of pastoral
care in Judaism and Catholicism.

We hope that the series will help ministers and church leaders
view afresh the theological and ethical foundations of care and
counseling. All of the books have a practical dimension, but even
more important than that, they help us see care and counseling
differently. Compared with writings of the last thirty years in this
field, some of the books will seem startlingly different. They will
need to be read and pondered with care. But I have little doubt that

the series will make a profound and lasting impact upon the way we understand and practice our care for one another.

In *The Family and Pastoral Care* Herbert Anderson presents the results of several years of research and experience in the care of families. His work with families has gained considerable attention across the country and amongst the membership of the American Association of Pastoral Counselors.

What Professor Anderson gives us here is not a theology of the family but a theology *for* the family—a broadly based theology that is relevant to life as a whole but especially pertinent to the particular needs of family life in the modern context. Working principally from the doctrine of creation, he celebrates the qualities of change, interdependence, and diversity of life as a whole and of the family in particular. And within this theological context he sets forth an engaging and highly useful theory of the five stages of the family life cycle.

At the more practical level, Professor Anderson works primarily out of a systems approach to family care, counseling, and intervention. Strong and healthy families are those with flexible roles, consistent and fair rules or maxims, and integrating rituals. Helpers need to concentrate on the entire family system, not just on individual members, recognizing circular as well as linear causality. They need to identify with the family while clearly remaining outside the system, be a genuine presence, have skills in redefining the problems that face the family, and understand ways of altering destructive alliances within the family.

Here is an unusual book that moves easily from theological interpretation to the details of practical intervention. It will go far to shape both our theological understanding of the family and our actual practice of supporting and strengthening this crucial social institution.

DON S. BROWNING

Introduction

SOURCES OF AUTHORITY
ON THE FAMILY

In one sense, everybody is an authority on the family. Each of us has an opinion on how to handle adolescents or aging parents or marital disputes. Our image of what the family should look like and how it should function is in part a composite of personal encounters, many of which are a continuation of patterns learned at home. Studying the family is therefore more than an objective exploration; it is a personal odyssey as well.

THE FAMILY OF ORIGIN

The family that raised us is our first and primary authority on the purpose, form, and function of family life. My own family of origin was a rather traditional company of four. My father was a busy parish pastor and my mother, after she married, did not work outside the home. I have a brother five years younger than myself.

From my father's side I inherited a strong tradition of independence which is captured by the Finnish word *siisuu,* meaning tenacity or dogged determination. It is that spirit that prompted my seventeenth-century ancestors to leave Finland for Sweden in order to transform forests into farmland. Centuries later that same lineage emigrated to North Dakota in order to tame the prairies. As I look at my own life, I sense that this spirit of dogged determination was not lost out there on the prairies.

My mother's side of the family was more tightly knit. For more than seventy years her siblings have maintained a powerfully supportive—yet confining—emotional network. Their relationships have been marked by the influence of a father who moved to a farm across the road from his mother and never differentiated from her. It is not easy for a member to leave my maternal family. It is equally difficult for anyone to marry into that family.

As I reflect on just those strands of my family inheritance, I am not surprised that it took me awhile to get married. By "getting married" I mean not only the ritual sense of the marriage ceremony itself but also the emotional bonding process that continues for some time after the wedding. I still struggle to achieve a balance between the rugged individualism of a prairie farmer and the close-building tendencies of a family that never left home. When Phyllis, my wife, began to prepare for a professional career, family tension about being separate and being together was sharpened in a new and sometimes painful way. We continue striving to learn how to live together separately without disregarding either the importance of autonomy or the necessity of community.

Watching our two children move all too quickly toward adulthood has provided another lesson in family living. It is not easy for parents to learn how to love their children deeply and also let them go. Even if we regard our children from birth on as unique persons, we still want to hold onto them more tightly than we should when they begin to claim for themselves the autonomy we have encouraged. Autonomy and community are not mutually exclusive, and the more we can believe that, the easier it is to let go of those we love. Letting them go, in turn, makes it easier for them to come home again. It is within the family that we learn, and continue to learn, the difficult but necessary art of being separate together.[1]

I invite you as a caring and helping person to make a pilgrimage to your family of origin as a part of your reading of this volume. You may want to recall, as I have, the dominant myths that support the family's history, as well as the stories that sustain those myths. Later on you might be prompted to remember the roles, rules, and rituals that kept the family together. But pilgrimage or not, our first experience of being in a family is clearly a primary authority for all of us on what families ought to be.

THE SOCIAL SCIENCES

Beyond our own personal experience there are also other sources of authority concerning the family. Prominent among them are the studies generated in recent years in the various disciplines of the social sciences.

Anthropologists in their studies of the family have sought to discover universal patterns that transcend societal and cultural boundaries. They have identified cross-cultural differences and similarities in family structure and in child-rearing practices. They have established the universality of the incest taboo and of the family's role in the process of maturation.

Sociological studies of the family have carefully examined such things as mate selection, role definition in marriage, and the significance of birth order in relation to vocational choice. Although sociologists are becoming more interested in optimal family functioning, they have still not given much attention to the elusive but important psychodynamics of interaction within the family.

Social historians have recently begun to examine the history of family life as a window into human history in general. The sources for such study are limited because most of the people who have given us a record of past events were men who knew little about women and children or about family life. Despite that limitation, social historians have been able to piece together an understanding of how the family has changed, and been changed by, evolving social needs. The social history of the family is a challenge to our nostalgia. It shows that while certain patterns have persisted, there is no one standard form. The family has endured precisely because of its capacity to change. It may even be of some comfort to realize that human beings have weathered periods of upheaval before now, even upheaval in their cherished views of living together in a family.

Anthropology, sociology, and social history have all contributed significantly to our modern understanding of family life. For me, however, the authority from the human sciences that I continue to find most helpful is that of systems theory. The systems approach to family therapy offers rich resources for the task of developing an understanding of effective family functioning as well as new methods of care for troubled families.

The Family as a Human System

The properties of the individual human organism and the vital features of the family as an organism have two things in common— the interdependence of parts and a specialization of function. Like the human body, the family functions best when the interdependence of each specialized part is maintained in appropriate balance;

that interdependence is of such a nature that one person or part of the system cannot change without affecting the whole. The family is unlike the human body, however, in that the specific parts or roles are not fixed; an eye cannot be a mouth, though the family listener can become the "speaker of the house."

The family as an organism or human system is a group, limited in membership, of human beings, who have regular interaction with one another over time. Family membership is determined by both external and internal boundaries. "Boundary" is a metaphor referring to an imaginary line that distinguishes between members and among systems. Ordinarily, membership in a family depends on such external determinants as marriage, birth, or adoption. The internal boundaries of a family are often unspoken; we become aware of them only after we have crossed them.

As a system, the whole of any family is greater than the sum of its parts. In that sense the family is like many other human systems that have a life of their own and hence their own history. We will examine later (in chapter 2) how the family moves through five epochs in its history, each of the five being characterized by a dominant theme that describes the principal task of the family as a unit during that period. Because each family has a life of its own, it is also possible to say that a family can get sick; and families are likely to become troubled if we bring into our new relationships the emotional baggage of unresolved issues from past family relationships.

The goal of the family as a human system is to maintain equilibrium. To that end it assigns roles, establishes rules, and preserves rituals that will help to restore or maintain systemic balance. Sometimes that equilibrium may be at the expense of one family member who is identified as the family problem or scapegoat. Even when patterns of personal interaction are painful or destructive of the family as a whole, the family may resist change in order to conserve familiar patterns.

Within the family as a system it is essential to keep a balance between the needs/demands of individuals and the needs/demands of the whole. Individual personality does not flourish where the individual is valued only as a unit of the system. Yet individuals do not reach their highest personal development unless they learn how to live together with others. If a family errs too much in the direction of individual needs, there is insufficient commitment to participation in the kind of community that fosters individual growth. If, on the other hand, there is too much togetherness and overinvolvement in the family, that can obstruct change and thereby impede individual growth. In the family a balance between individuation and participation is necessary in order that people may learn how to live together separately.

THE FAMILY AND THE
JUDEO-CHRISTIAN TRADITION

The Bible discloses a rich history of complexity and diversity in family life. The Old Testament in particular is filled with descriptive stories of sibling rivalry and incest, enduring covenants and unfaithfulness, marital deceit and family loyalty—all of which chronicle a variety of family patterns or structures.

Old Testament prescriptions about the family include proverbial bits of wisdom on marriage and parenting as well as levitical laws regarding sexual purity in the family. These patterns of family action are not directly applicable to modern cultures. For example, it would be difficult to reinstate the levirate practice that requires a surviving brother to father children for his brother's widow as a way of insuring that the widow will be without the shame of childlessness and the dead man's name will not "perish from the earth." That pattern of family life did provide care, but it was bound to the social presuppositions and needs of its particular time.

New Testament teachings about the family are more contradictory than diverse. While Jesus accepted and even guarded the family, he refused to absolutize it. For Jesus, participation in the realm of God required the subordination of all human commitments to that higher loyalty. Although the family was affirmed as necessary, its significance was limited. By the time of Paul, however, the radical, world-disturbing spirit of Jesus had already been replaced by an emphasis on structure. Christians needed to be seen as favoring stability. Pauline references to submission, love, honor, and obedience are therefore related to the promotion of order. New Testament prescriptions about family life are always set forth in terms of the cultural formulations of its time. We take the Bible seriously when we regard it as a historical document which is itself constantly involved in a struggle to express God's care for the world. It is inevitable, though, that forms of family care change over the years because they are as much responsive to human need as they are reflective of the enduring nature of God.

The church's attitude toward the family has also changed through the centuries as new social circumstances brought forth new needs to be met. Born in the sixteenth century in order to meet the social circumstances of that time, the Protestant family was new in the history of Christianity. The medieval church, Luther insisted, had canonized those who withdrew from the world into cloisters, but the real saints are those who put up with squalling babies, shrewish wives, and drunken husbands. Participation in the family rather than the cloister became, for the Reformation, the new norm for Christian faithfulness. Because God gives us children, bringing them up to serve God is, for Luther, the noblest and most precious work on earth.[2]

About the middle of the nineteenth century another shift in the family occurred with the onset of the industrial revolution. The living room was split off geographically from the office and factory. As a result, there were sharper differences between husband and wife as regards status, roles, and responsibilities. The family continued to be a school for public service, but it became also a refuge from the world. In the family mothers and children were protected from the demanding pressures and dark temptations of the larger world. The family was also a refuge into which fathers could retreat for renewal and fortification. "In myth and reality, the Puritan family of community gave way to the Victorian family of refuge, the new family that sanctioned and sanctified the realities of 19th century America."[3] The tension between Luther's vision of the family (as a nursery for learning about Christian service) and the Victorian family as a refuge from a harsh world still remains.

A Theology for the Family

Because the family continues to change in order to meet new social circumstances, it is impossible to insist on only one particular form of family as normative for all times and cultures. This fact of inevitable diversity means that theologically normative statements about the family are most accurate when they are paradoxical. In order to articulate a perspective that is consistent with this paradoxical character of the Christian tradition, but also free to engage seriously the human sciences, I am proposing as the third authority for this study—in addition to personal experience and scholarly studies in the social sciences—a theology for the family.

A theology for the family begins by identifying themes from the whole of the Christian tradition that are of particular significance for understanding the family. Such an approach seeks to avoid absolutizing either the family or the theological tradition. It allows for the possibility of a lively interaction between Christian texts/traditions and common human experience. A theology for the family begins by exploring general theological principles—order, change, uniqueness, mutuality, justice, forgiveness, diversity—in order to understand first of all what it means to live in a family. The pastoral theologian's agenda is not to identify a "Christian family" but to help people find ways of being Christian in families.

Creation and the Realm of God
—A Paradox of Loyalties

Two paradoxes have already been suggested. First, family involves a delicate balance between attention to the individual and attention to the unit as a whole; the health and vitality of a family is finally determined by how its members learn to be separate together. The second dialectic has to do with the interaction between the family and environment. A family is a haven or place of retreat from the storms and pressures of the world around; at the same time, the family does not and cannot exist for its own sake. As a human system, it must be both open and closed—capable of trafficking easily with its many environments and able to shut out the demands and clamor of the world in order to create a moment's peace.

A theology for the family is shaped by two similarly contradictory principles. First, the family is a necessary component of creation. Despite wide diversity of form and function throughout human history, the family has fulfilled God's intent to provide a context for creation and care in order to insure the continuity of the human species. From this theological perspective we simply affirm as God's intention what is chronicled in anthropological studies: There is no known human community without family in some form. It is in the nature of things that people live together in those communities that we have labeled family. This theological affirmation is rooted more in an understanding of God as the one who cares than in any particular biblical passage prescribing the existence of the family. The Bible simply presupposes the family as a basic social unit and everywhere acknowledges its importance.

Second, the importance of the family is qualified by the teaching of Jesus. From the perspective of discipleship, the family cannot be an end in itself. The metaphor of the realm of God is used here to point to God's intervention in history for purposes of continuing a process of transformation begun in creation. We are invited to participate in that process. Being a disciple in God's realm means being a subject who is willing to function as a sign to the world of God's vision for creation. The realm of God is both gift and task. It comes to us by God's grace, not by human effort, and it sends us on a quest for justice, peace, and freedom in ever-widening human communities.

These claims of the gospel for a radical loyalty that transcends familial bonding are tempered by the recognition that we continue to be creatures in creation and members of a particular society. Everybody needs to belong somewhere. What we call the family continues to be the place where God locates human beings in creation. Yet the family that turns inward loses its moral fiber. Inherent in the Christian tradition, therefore, is a healthy tension of perspectives that guards against a variety of false uses of the family. The family is affirmed as necessary for human life to continue—*and* its significance is limited. Ties to the family cannot be dissolved capriciously, even for the sake of the gospel—*and* yet for the sake of God's realm ties to the family are definitely relativized.

From the perspective of creation, then, we gather insights for determining what the family ought to look like. From the perspective of God's realm, however, we gain clarity regarding the family's place in the service of all humanity. Both perspectives affect the ways in which families function. From the perspective of creation, care and criticism are mandated; from the perspective of discipleship, it is essential that the family encourage individuation in order that people might become autonomous enough to leave home for the sake of the gospel.

A LOOK AHEAD

This volume has two parts. Part One outlines a theology for the family. Because purpose and form are reciprocally linked, this theological development will alternate between the three fundamental *purposes* of the family (procreation, community, and individuation) and three essential characteristics of family *structure* (change, interdependence, and diversity). The argument proceeds in the following manner:

- Procreation, indeed any addition to a family unit (either in membership or function), produces change.

- The capacity to adapt to *change* is essential for the family's survival in relation to society as a whole and as a particular organism.

- The family is a stabilizing *community* that provides continuity in the midst of change.

- The vitality of the family, however, depends on an openness to its environment and on the *interdependence* of its membership.

- The focus of a family on *individuation* fosters the uniqueness of each member; never an end in itself, the family exists for the sake of individual growth.

- The promotion of individual growth within a family leads to a *diversity* within the family that is paralleled in the variety of family structures within society; such diversity is a sign of God's extravagance.

In each instance, the family looks beyond itself. It exists so that the human community might endure, societies be stabilized, and individuals be prepared to serve the wider human community.

What is necessary for family structures in relation to the larger society or created order is also essential for each individual family unit. Individual families flourish and foster the kind of community necessary for individuation if they can adapt to change, maintain interdependence, and celebrate or at least tolerate diversity.

Although connections between a general theological perspective and our pastoral work with families in particular are made throughout, Part Two of this volume will focus specifically on issues in the pastoral care of families. We ask, first, how families function, because what is normative for effective family functioning not only helps to make explicit the goals of pastoral work but also provides clues about how families become troubled. The dialectic between what is required from creation and what is promised by the gospel is more sharply defined in the family's functioning.

Since this is a book about pastoral care, the principles set forth in the closing chapter, although influenced by a systems approach, have implications for general pastoral work in which care is the focus. No other helping professional has the kind of access to people in families that pastors do. This does not mean that we all should become family therapists. There are, however, an infinite variety of ordinary moments in our pastoral care with families in which an appropriate response may help effect change. My hope is thus that the book as a whole will contribute to the development of a theology for the family, enhance the capacity to think interactionally or systemically about people, and foster confidence for the ongoing pastoral care of families.

PART ONE

A THEOLOGY
FOR THE FAMILY

CHAPTER 1

The Family
and
Procreation

Mark is a paraplegic. Before he and Carla decided to marry they had talked together extensively about his impotence and about adoption. For them, natural procreation was impossible; yet both wanted to raise children. Carla had even conferred privately with a counselor about the possibility of artificial insemination using the sperm of Mark's brother. Neither Mark nor Carla was prepared for the priest's refusal to marry them in the church.

Even before they were married Carolyn knew that Jeff liked to spend time with his male friends; much of their brief courtship in fact had been spent in the company of Jeff's buddies. Recently Carolyn was finding herself more and more alone, always waiting for Jeff. Her delight at being pregnant was understandable: at last she would have an affectionate companion around at all times, someone who would not leave her. Within two years of the baby's arrival, Carolyn was persuaded by her pastor to join a support group made up of parents who had participated in child abuse.

Cecile had long borne the scars of sexual abuse by her father: she protected herself from men by overeating and overweight. It represented a significant victory over personal and financial obstacles when she completed training for a career in the medical field—and at the same time lost considerable weight. Still determined not to marry, Cecile wanted very much to have a child. In consultation with a physician she had already completed plans for artificial insemination when she called for a conference with the pastor.

Gary and Anne were both looking forward to marriage as soon as they graduated from college. The conflict between them stemmed primarily from Gary's reluctance for "career reasons" to have children. Although Anne was herself preparing for a career in law, she was less certain about not wanting to have children. Gary's insistence on having a vasectomy as a condition for marriage precipitated an extended series of premarital conferences with the pastor. Gary finally agreed to delay the vasectomy until five years after the marriage, but he remained adamant about not having any children.

PROCREATION AS PURPOSE

The family in any society serves multiple purposes. High among them is the responsibility of procreation. The family is also expected to provide for the nurturance and protection of the young. This universal purpose of having and rearing children transcends cultural and historical particularities. It reflects the way humans in all times and places have cared for the future.

In human societies the marital partnership is the primary agent of procreation. Yet because of the long period of dependency that characterizes human development, the family as a whole must be regarded as that unit of society which has the responsibility for maintaining the future of human generations. In fulfilling that responsibility the family participates in the continuing creative activity of God.

Creativity and Biology

Whether and how the family participates in God's ongoing creation is much debated among Christians. Until recently the questions clustered around whether it was ethically appropriate to interfere with the natural processes of reproduction in order to prevent conception. The priest's refusal to marry Mark and Carla represents an extreme extension of the conviction that biology is God's natural law for procreation.

Human mating, however, has always been more than a merely biological affair. Today especially, procreation has become increasingly intentional. The cases of Carolyn and Cecile—for very different reasons—add to the question of intentionality in the procreative process other questions about psychological need and personal right. The struggle between Gary and Anne is further consequence of the new freedom afforded by modern reproductive technology. If procreation remains one of the primary purposes of the family, then we must ask whether and under what circumstances it is appropriate to marry and *not* have children.

The biblical admonition to be fruitful and multiply (Gen. 1:28) makes explicit what is already implicit in the reproductive process of creation. Because human beings must be *admonished* to procreate, it can be assumed that participation in the reproductive process, like mating itself, has always involved more than simple instinct. Mating always assumes a self-conscious intention, even when the mating couple does not make the deliberate choice. Similarly, impregnation has always been the consequence of an intentional act even though precise knowledge of the procreative process is a relatively modern phenomenon. Because of recently acquired knowledge, couples who marry today are faced with choices not possible or necessary as recently as a century ago.

For much of human history, high birth rates were not so much the outcome of ignorance as a requirement for survival—necessary in order to insure an adequate work force in the face of the ravages of disease and war. Procreation was obviously essential for the continuation of the species. The assumed connection between mating and procreation was thus understandable. Modern technology, however, has made that connection less obvious in two ways: In most countries it is no longer necessary to make lots of babies in order to insure that one or two might survive to adulthood. And because of industrialization the production of offspring is now no longer an economic necessity. Biological accident, therefore, can no longer be automatically equated with God's purpose.

Creativity and Psychology

If procreation is an intentional act, neither an inevitable consequence of mating nor a necessity for survival, then the question of motivation becomes critical. It is not enough to say, as some have said, that every child needs to be wanted. Children have been wanted for a wide variety of reasons, not all of which are in the child's best interests. Sometimes children have been conceived in the hope of saving a marriage, or in order to appease a grandparent, or out of obedience to church law, or to preserve a family name. Sometimes children are born so that men can establish their potency, or so that women may experience a kind of fulfillment in childbirth. Carolyn's abuse of her child was the result of frustration and rage: The child had failed to fulfill her need for an affectionate companion. Today more than ever it is clear that parenthood must first of all be an act of altruism. The fathers and mothers most effective at nurturing are those whose children are not conceived in order to meet personal needs.

Questions about needs, wants, and rights in the matter of procreation have likewise been intensified by the new technology of reproduction. Dependable contraception has made it possible for women to experience a newfound freedom from the restrictions of parenthood such as men have always known. On the other hand, artificial means of impregnation have made it possible for virtually every woman, if she wishes, to have a child. Is such desire or need enough? Is having a child a right as well as a responsibility?

Creativity and Theology

In a carefully argued report on "Choices in Childlessness" sponsored by the British Council of Churches it is suggested that the right to have children can "never be argued in isolation from a child's right to a good parenting."[1] Procreation is not a right independent of that caring context ordinarily identified as family. It is rather a gift of God and a service offered to the human community.

Of course the acknowledgement that children are a gift does not eliminate all human responsibility with respect to the procreative process; neither does it imply that children are gifts in any ordinary sense of the term—something to be possessed and used. From a Christian point of view, the having and rearing of children is itself an expression of faith, hope, and love. When we say that children are a gift, that affirmation is grounded in the conviction that "in giving us children God also wills to give us himself."[2] As gift, children are one way that God continues to care for creation. The act of procreation is a reminder that the family exists not for its own sake but in order to serve the wider human community.

The new covenant in Christ alters this emphasis on procreation in two ways. First, membership in the covenant community is by faith and baptism rather than by birth and circumcision; that too is God's creation. Second, the expectation of the advent of God's rule modifies the necessity for humans to insure the continuity of humankind in general, or leave behind personal offspring as a heritage in particular. As members of the covenant community, we are an eschatological people here in the midst of creation. From that perspective, readiness for the coming reign of God is more important than having and rearing children. Christians who marry may for the sake of discipleship choose *not* to have children.

The new covenant is created and sustained by the sovereign power of God. And yet the future of generations still depends on the family acting cooperatively with God in the creative process. Even though responsible creativity may mean that some families will be childless for the sake of discipleship, procreation must remain one of the family's purposes and one of the means by which humankind participates in God's ongoing creative activity.

CREATIVITY AND THE CRISIS OF PERSPECTIVE

The practical application of this dialectic between creation and discipleship is complicated today by two opposing issues. There is first the matter of controlling the world's population growth, which is a global ethical problem. The poverty and famine that plague many countries are consequences of overpopulation. The survival of humankind is in part dependent on careful managing of the growth of population throughout the world. The capacity to nurture the young is mandated by creation as surely as the necessity to procreate. The desire for children is thus qualified by the needs of the larger community to limit population growth.

Among the more developed countries there is another tendency that runs in the opposite direction. In its extreme form, this tendency regards children as an impediment to self-fulfillment. Men and women who regard their careers, or the accumulation of wealth, or the freedom for leisure activity as primary are sometimes reluctant to encumber their lives with children. Gary's reluctance to have children reflects this trend. The decision not to have children may be prompted more by a truncated perspective on the future than by a commitment to Christian discipleship.

The crisis of perspective facing the family today is in one sense the logical outcome of the industrial and technological revolutions. If the family is no longer perceived as the agent primarily responsible either for production or for reproduction, it would seem not to have any inherent reason for giving attention to the needs of the next generation. If responsibility for the existence and well-being of future generations belongs to the larger society, the family can be content to retreat from the world and occupy itself simply with the present satisfaction of emotional needs.

The evidence for this loss of future perspective is considerable. It can be seen in the remoteness of parents who, having little to transmit to the next generation, give priority to their own self-fulfillment; increasingly children are suffering more from emotional neglect than from the smothering embrace. Moreover, there is a growing segment of society that not only neglects and fears children, but regards them as a nuisance, an obstacle to personal freedom and satisfaction.

> Neither Bob nor Barbara had custody of the children from their previous marriages who came to visit them every other weekend. Only recently married, the couple sought counseling because they found themselves unable to manage the children when they did visit. Both partners wanted, when the children were with them, to create a new merged family, yet they both treated their own children (all under the age of eleven) as guests rather than as family. Both also became angry when the children did not respond with appropriate gratitude. The resentment Bob and Barbara felt toward their own children for not behaving as proper guests illustrates a thinly veiled parental detachment.

In order to counter current trends in family life that reflect the absence of a future perspective, a theology for the family must be rooted in an understanding of creation whereby men and women are intentional participants with God in the procreative process. The demands of Christian discipleship, while they may relativize our procreative obligations from creation, do not eliminate them. The family is that agency in creation that has as one of its purposes the continuity of the human community.

THE ETHICS OF PROCREATION
AND PASTORAL CARE

Questions about a family's participation in the procreative process are almost inevitable in pastoral work. They are likely to emerge at the following times: (1) in premarital conversation; (2) when there is a so-called problem pregnancy; and (3) when a childless couple desires the assistance of medical technology in order to have a child.

Premarital Conversation

Because it can no longer be assumed that every couple who marries will want children, it is useful in premarital work to build in questions about having children. The most natural occasion for that discussion is during consideration of the wedding service. During the wedding, prayers may or may not be offered for the gift of children.

> Keith and Marilyn had been living together for nearly five years before Marilyn agreed to marry. Her caution grew out of her own family history and a personal odyssey marked by a great deal of instability. Keith had understood her reasons for not wanting to get married, but was surprised to hear from Marilyn that she also did not want to have children for some time—if ever. The issue was never resolved. The matter of Marilyn's career, coupled with her unwillingness to have children, were factors in the undoing of the marriage.

It is most important already at the beginning of a marital relationship that the couple be of a common mind on this matter. Had the counseling pastor been more insistent in the case of Keith and Marilyn, the couple might have resolved the issue without divorce.

Procreative responsibilities include nurture as well as birth. Settling the matter of having children is only half the battle. Decision must also be made as to who will have primary responsibility for raising the children. It can no longer be assumed that the woman will be the one to set aside her career in order to raise a family. A number of other options are available by which parents may exercise their responsibility to provide for the care and nurture of children. How the care of the children will be managed needs to be understood as a part of the larger question about procreation. The diversity of child-rearing options today has increased the necessity for the marital pair to be intentional about the parenting role.

Problem Pregnancies

The issues surrounding the beginning of human life are complex and emotionally charged. Counseling with couples or individuals regarding abortion or medical procedures such as amniocentesis and gender-selection involves a delicate blending of the ethical and psychological factors relating to responsible creativity. The choices that people must make in such circumstances are seldom eased by an appeal to rights. The gift of children must always be understood in the light of the Christian's obligations to ever-larger human communities.

> After their second child died in infancy Tom and Carol sought both a medical assessment and pastoral assistance before attempting another pregnancy. The medical assessment was that another pregnancy would involve some risk. They were encouraged to decide before Carol became pregnant again whether they would have amniocentesis and how they would respond if the test results were negative. With the help of their pastor, the couple decided that they did not want to risk another problematic pregnancy.

Whatever the decision, problems in relation to pregnancy and birth become a part of the family's emotional history. In order to keep an abortion or an illegitimate pregnancy secret, some families develop an elaborate conspiracy of silence that eventually becomes a way of life. Miscarriages and stillbirths often generate a secret grief that gains in emotional power over a period of time. In working with people for whom a problem pregnancy or birth has occurred, counselors can help to place the matter in a larger family context. This is not done punitively but in order to assure that any decision made will have an explicit place in the family's history for the sake of succeeding generations.

New Procreative Procedures

In the case of childless couples who wish to have children, the Christian community can help them find their way through the labyrinth of complicated ethical questions created by the new reproductive technology. Advances in medical science are a sign of hope for people who have been unable to have children by natural means. In general, the use of appropriate artificial means to enhance the possibility of conception is ethically acceptable. The ethical appropriateness of procedures such as artificial insemination, *in vitro* fertilization, and surrogate motherhood is modified by the principle that the family has primary responsibility for the procreative process. Couples who wish to have children but are impeded physically from doing so need the support of the Christian community in overcoming those impediments by appropriate artificial means.

The obligations from creation for procreation, however, cannot be transformed into rights. The family is the responsible partner in the ongoing creative activity of God, but life is finally a gift from God. Having children is not a right. Because couples are often eager to use any means to overcome impediments to childbearing, the pastor's task is to mediate between ethical understanding and medical possibility in ways that include the moral and psychological consequences for each individual, for families, and for the larger human community.

CHAPTER 2

Change—A Sign That God Is Making Something New

As we outline a theology for the family in Part One we will be discussing in alternate chapters three purposes of the family and three essential characteristics of family form or structure. Having dealt with the purpose of procreation we speak now of the form of change.

CHANGE AND ADAPTABILITY

The birth of a child is a gift, but it also poses a problem for the family as a system. The addition of one or more children to a family represents the kind of change that in turn requires further adaptation. The procreative purpose of the family is most effectively fulfilled, therefore, within a human system that is able to adapt to the changes that result from the addition of new members.

Because the family is an interactional system, any change in its membership or function affects the whole. When the first child is added, the marital dyad must change in order to take into account the presence of another member. Each additional member magnifies the complexity of the family as a human system. The fact that people change as they grow up and grow older also makes accommodation an ongoing necessity. The capacity to adapt to all such changes is essential for each particular family's survival.

The family as a structure in society has also changed and continues to change in relation to its environment. The picture that emerges from nearly every survey of the family's history is one of change and adaptability—"a kind of controlled disorder that varies in accordance with pressing social and economic needs. The complexities, conflicts in roles, and variations imposed on individuals in modern society require an even greater diversity and malleability."[1] What is required of the family today is what has always been necessary for its survival—adaptability to change.

The capacity to adapt is more than a necessity for survival; it is the mark of being human in creation. The willingness to make the efforts required for growth through creative adaptation is what makes it possible for humankind to live under a wide range of conditions and create immensely diverse ways of life. Because the family as a structure in creation is also itself in the process of becoming something new, it is not even desirable that its form remain static.

Human beings and human structures are more than objects of change. They are also subjects of change. Within the long process of evolutionary development, the human species has been a subject that interacts with biological and sociocultural forces to effect change. Human development is a continuing process of creating and being created; the process is never finished. The family as a human institution in history is similarly both subject and object, effecting change and being affected by changes in its environment.[2] The family as a system changes as it is changed, and it too is not yet finished.

Because of the rapid process of changes that is likely to continue to shape modern societies, Theodore Lidz is probably correct in suggesting that adaptability is essential for individual and family life. "Adaptability," he says, "requires an ability to utilize intellect to plan toward the changing future rather than a need to adhere to ways inculcated in childhood or the patterns of parents' lives."[3] Equilibrium within the family is therefore achieved only by recognizing change as constant—the highest form of stability.

MAKING SOMETHING NEW

The changes that occur in and to the family are characteristic of the whole creation. Nothing that lives is static. All of life is caught up in motion and change. And because God is still creating, nothing that lives is finished or complete. To believe in a living God is to recognize change as an inevitable dimension of life. Adapting to change is therefore a creative act as well as a necessity for survival. Change, as a motif from creation, is hence characteristic also of family structure, both in relation to society and within the family itself.

The Christian believes that the future toward which God is drawing us is always new. Teilhard de Chardin is correct in insisting that "we must distinctly and once for all finish with the legend that continually crops up again of an earth that has, in man and with the man we now see, reached the limit of its biological potentialities."[4] God is not done with us yet. If we formulate the future strictly on the basis of the present or the past, we prematurely restrict the future of that humankind which God is continually making new. Change is an indisputable element of creation.

God is not finished with the family either. As an institution, it continues to participate in the changing character of all reality. Although there is no known society that does not have a family structure, there is also no single image of family that has served or will serve all the various cultures and communities with their diverse needs. The future of the family is thus open, not just in response to the diversity of needs but because God is acting to make something new.

God's creation cannot be a finished product because what God is making new is also being destroyed. In the family this happens when out of fear we seek to replicate the future on the basis of the past. It happens when families seek to minimize change by cluttering the future with heirlooms and rigid rules. Sometimes the fear of something new generates change that is destructive of people and communities. For example, a family's fear of change may prompt it to sacrifice the growth, development, and emerging freedom of one of its members for the stability of "things as they used to be." The Creator must "constantly make new" in order to counter our efforts to diminish God's creative work by limiting change.

Change is often perceived as frightening or dangerous because it produces difference. It is not always easy to live with the rich diversity of modern environments. William James has aptly observed that only those capable of living the strenuous life can endure the conflict and energies unleashed by diversity and change.[5] Both are as disruptive as they are indisputable. Particular families under stress often seek to return to another time in the family's history when "things were better." Or a family may romanticize a time in the past in order to cope with the pain or stress of the present. The effect is to limit the possibilities of change for the future.

The inability to cope with change and loss produces what Norman Paul has described as a "family style that is variably unresponsive to a wide range of changes, including our losses and disappointments. Such unresponsiveness is expressed in attempts to deny the passage of time; these often bring about the family's unwillingly keeping one of its members in an inappropriately dependent position."[6]

The family returns to this relatively fixed state when it is disturbed or under stress. Growth and change are severely restricted. Dependency of family members is enforced in order to minimize loss. Something old and familiar is enforced in order to prevent God from making something new.

THE CONSTANTLY CHANGING FAMILY

The fact that the family has changed and changed and changed again in the course of human history does not dispel our worry about current changes in the structure of the family. Many regard the changes in family life today as an erosion of the honored traditions and family patterns that once formed the family as an institution superordinate to its individual members. It was assumed that the whole was more important than its parts. The new direction, which I have labeled "being separate together," seeks a balance between individual and institutional well-being. The remarkable contribution of systems theory is that the consideration of the whole family as an interdependent human system makes it easier to see each part more clearly.

From the start, the human animal has had particular needs for the safety of a family structure, or something like it, because of the human infant's protracted vulnerability and slow maturation to adulthood. A nurturing and protecting environment is essential for Homo sapiens because human instincts are culturally derived and human childhood so long protracted. Whatever changes have occurred in the structure of the family, the need for a safe space in which its younger members can grow has remained constant.

Some of the changes that have occurred in the structure and function of the family are noted here because they impinge on major themes considered in this volume. Not all of these changes, of course, have enhanced the family's capacity to provide a lively context for human growth.

1. The recognition of individual autonomy and of the right to personal freedom in the pursuit of happiness may well be the most important change in the family over the last centuries. It has been a change from distance, deference, and patriarchy to what has been called affective individualism. The importance of individual autonomy, and the corresponding respect for individual rights within limits set by the need for social cohesion, emerged in the late seventeenth and early eighteenth centuries both in England and New England. Among middle- and upperclass families, this change resulted in a trend toward greater freedom for children, a more equal partnership for husbands and wives, and a walling off of the nuclear family from both interference and support either from kin or from the larger community.[7] This trend toward affective individualism has significantly moved the modern family toward emotional isolation.

2. The close interdependent relationship with its environment that characterized the traditional family has been replaced on the one hand by isolation but on the other hand by greater dependence on the larger society for that which the family consumes. As ties to the outside world have weakened, the emotional bonds of family members to each other have intensified. The family's necessary openness to the world around it has been hedged about by a privatization that regards the environment as a hostile or intrusive force from which the family must be protected. Despite widespread evidence of violence within the family, evil is thought of as existing only outside the family.

3. The forming of families is not only more freely intentional today, but it is also based more on affection than on economic need or political opportunism.. When romantic love, maternal love, and domesticity became norms for the family, property and lineage gave way to personal happiness and individual self-development as criteria for choosing a marriage partner. In *The Making of the Modern Family* Edward Shorter sets forth the thesis that the family today is a consequence of this shift toward "sentiment," which makes personal happiness and emotional ties to other people the principal criteria for ordering the objectives of the family.[8]

The changes noted above have enhanced human freedom and autonomy in the family and have increased the importance of emotional bonding among its members. However, other changes, brought about largely because of the industrial revolutions, have moved the family to become increasingly isolated from its environment.

The family cannot now endure, nor could it ever endure, as an isolated unit cut off from larger structures of support. The family that retreats from the world quickly ceases to be adaptable. It resists change. For that reason, interdependence and diversity, along with change, must be regarded as themes from creation that are essential for the family as a structure of creation. As a human system, the family must be characterized by the acceptance of diversity, adaptability to change, and a commitment to a community life that is marked by mutuality and interdependence.

THE FAMILY LIFE CYCLE:
FIVE EPOCHS OF CHANGE

The capacity to adapt, which is necessary for the family to endure as an institution in society, is equally essential for the survival of particular families. The membership of the family changes and its needs change as a consequence of its changing circumstances. Sometimes these changes occur in a relatively predictable way according to the family's life cycle. At other times changes are the result of unanticipated loss due to separation, divorce, or death. As an organism that itself changes, the family creates a context that fosters individual change. The family as a social system changes according to its own history of changing tasks.

There are five major epochs in the family's history, as suggested in the table below. Each epoch is marked by a predictable crisis of change on account of which the family must adapt in ways that will continue both individual growth and communal accessibility. Individual transitions into and out of different family roles—such as leaving home, getting married, becoming parents, coping with widowhood—are all interrelated with changes in the family as a system. The capacity of the family to accept these changes will in time enhance the capacity of individuals within the system to move through their developmental process with a minimum of difficulty.

Epoch	Period
Forming the family	From mate selection through early marriage
Enlarging the family	From the birth of children to their beginning school
Expanding the family	During school years
Extending the family	From the time the first child leaves
Re-forming the family	From the time the last child leaves through retirement

Epoch 1: Forming the Family

Leaving one's father and mother in order to form a new family requires a change of loyalty and role identity that is never easy. The capacity to establish the emotional boundaries necessary for marital intimacy and effective family functioning is dependent on the ability to differentiate oneself from one's family of origin. One is no longer primarily son or daughter but husband or wife. Because individual autonomy within community characterizes modern life both inside and outside the family, leaving home emotionally is essential today in forming a new family.

In order to be married it is necessary to divorce one's parents. That is a psychological transliteration of the biblical admonition: You must leave before you can cleave (Gen. 2:24). Living together separately requires clear but permeable boundaries between the generations. Pastoral work with couples prior to marriage is most effective when the focus is on leaving home and clarifying the boundaries of the newly forming family system.

The other aspect of forming a family is bonding. Bonding is the emotional process of "joining the marriage" that necessitates commitment and covenanting. It is unfortunate that some couples get divorced even before they have ever joined the marriage.

Epoch 2: Enlarging the Family

The addition of children during the epoch of enlarging the family evokes role changes. The role of parent is added to the marital role. The family as a system is likely to be troubled if biological fathers and mothers are unwilling to accept the role of parents and to change the patterns of interaction and boundaries within the system accordingly. But because this time of childrearing has become proportionately a smaller segment of one's life, it is essential for families that marital role identity be kept alive even during the time that parenting is central.

Families need parents who are "crazy enough about kids" to create the kind of atmosphere in which individuals can grow and flourish. It is generally unhealthy if the environment into which children are born has no room for them or is merely a vacuum they are expected to fill. A favorable space for growth is created by an intimacy that balances distance and closeness.[9]

The family changes each time a new person is added. Ordinarily the consequent adaptations are made naturally by the system. If, however, a family system is not reconstituted with each addition, then the family is likely to restrict ordinary developmental change in order to stay in balance.

Epoch 3: Expanding the Family

During the epoch of expanding the family the changes that occur are more emotional than structural. The family as a system needs to create an expanded context in order to accommodate the new ideas, feelings, and roles that accompany the individual growth of children and parents. This period is often a time of great stress in the family because everybody and everything seem to be changing. Roles and rules and rituals all change rapidly in order that the family as a system can create enough freedom for the growth of parents and children alike.

Within the family not all change in individuals is permanent or even for the better. Because the family constitutes a context for criticism as well as care, there should be freedom to critique change. And even when change is celebrated as a sign of life there also needs to be room for grieving those experiences of change perceived as loss. Some families try to prevent change in order to avoid grief. If a family cannot expand to make room for the changes that accompany growth, it is not surprising that some of its individual members feel they must leave the family in order to become what they might best become.

Epoch 4: Extending the Family

As the family is extended, the system changes again. This epoch generally begins when the first child leaves home and lasts until the last child is settled outside the home. It is a time for leaving and for letting go. Letting children go is sometimes as difficult for parents as leaving home is for children. Both parents and children need to understand that leaving is not the end of loving. The way we are able to leave home will determine the ease with which we can go home again.

Every time someone leaves the family, the system needs to readjust. Even though children always remain the parents' children, they primarily belong somewhere else. For that reason, the metaphor of extension is most appropriate. The family is most likely to remain connected if it can understand Mary's sojourn in Borneo and Millard's assignment to Albuquerque as extensions of the family. The family is where its members are.

Epoch 5: Re-forming the Family

The changes that accompany this final epoch in the family's life cycle include two role shifts. One is the acceptance of the grandparent role (which is often a jolt for those who skipped parenting), and the other is a return to the marital dyad as primary. The image of the "empty nest" is much too negative for this epoch. It implies that families are only for children. The family of origin is re-forming itself during this epoch as new family units are being formed. If the family has expanded and extended itself along the way, there is generally room enough for everyone.

The new intimacy between mother and father creates freedom

enough for everyone. Parents are too busy with each other to become overinvolved with their children, and children devote their energies to forming a new family without having to worry about parents. If it has been closed to change, the family as a system will often insist on loyalty to the original unit, and that can complicate the process of forming new families which in turn sets a new family life cycle in motion.

Although the changes that occur throughout the family's history are expected, they are no less traumatic when they occur. The capacity to grieve, even over the predictable losses that these changes produce, can help a family survive.

The family functions much like an accordion, expanding and contracting in accordance with changing family needs and external conditions. This has always been true, even when the family was larger in size and the space in which the family lived was smaller. The demands of modern society on individuals and on families simply require more diverse patterns of transition between epochs, and increased adaptability within each epoch, so that the family can continue to be a vital context for nurture and change.

UNANTICIPATED CHANGE

The family's need for adaptability to change is not limited to the predictable transitions of these five epochs. It is sometimes seriously tested by an unexpected loss—fire, theft, divorce, death. The family as a system will need to grieve for each such loss. Its adaptation will need to include that traumatic loss as a part of the family's memory. An unwillingness to do so limits the family's adaptability.

The family as a system also needs to adapt to the temporary loss of a family member due to a prolonged hospitalization or other lengthy separation. Sometimes it is more difficult for the family to adapt to an individual's return than to adjust to that individual's absence.

Changes brought about by divorce are sometimes overwhelming. The shift from a two-parent family to a one-parent family, perhaps even to a multiple-parent family, involves a delicate and usually difficult process of role adaptation, renegotiating boundaries, and determining membership as well as modifying interactional patterns and family self-understanding. The new family's adaptability cannot depend on previously established rituals of transition. The process of adaptation is complicated further by the presence of grief in a remarried or postinitial family.

Death is an upheaval from which some families never fully recover. The death of a parent, spouse, or child creates an emptiness in the system as well as in the lives of individual family members. Everything changes when someone in a family dies. Most grief work is appropriately concerned about the impact of the loss on individuals. Each individual's grief is uniquely shaped by his or her relationship to the deceased person. While it is important that pastoral work continue this individual focus, it is also necessary to recognize the grief that the system as such experiences. The family, as an organism with a life of its own, grieves the loss of one of its members. And the family as a whole must adjust its life to take into account the loss of one of its members.

Change and adaptability are inescapable dimensions of all of life. The family as an institution has demonstrated remarkable resilience in surviving the changes it has endured through human history. The capacity of the family to adapt to change has been one of the reasons for its survival. Adaptability to change is also an essential characteristic of each individual family unit. People change and families too must therefore change. Some of the changes are predictable in terms of the human life cycle as children grow up and leave home and adults grow older. Other changes are less anticipated but equally disruptive.

Everything that lives changes. Families remain vital as long as they can adapt to the changes that occur. Because we are fearful creatures we may resist change, preferring familiarity or presumed stability. By that action we not only prevent human growth; we may overlook what God is making new. The capacity to adapt to change is grounded in the confidence that all of creation, including the family, finds its continuity in God's constant re-creation.

CHAPTER 3

The Family
and
Social Stability

Change is a part of creation; continuity is a human need. Individuals and human systems alike seek to maintain continuity in the midst of change. Change that is perceived to be "too much" generates anxiety because the future seems too open. Out of that fear human beings act to increase continuity and decrease change. We remember the past as it never was with the hope that it might be like that again. We fix rules or establish patterns to insure that tomorrow will at least be continuous with today. We are willing to trade the freedom to grow and change for the security of knowing that things will be like they have always been.

It had not been easy for Jack and Rosemary Griffin to accept the fact that their eldest son Peter had joined a religious sect while attending the state university. The family had been Baptists for five generations. Great-grandfather Griffin had been a missionary to the Cherokee Indians and died heroically in a prairie fire. Rosemary's family tradition included several Baptist ministers. Being a Griffin and being a Baptist were synonymous. As a consequence of Peter's change in religious affiliation, Jack and Rosemary determined that none of the other three children would receive financial support unless they attended Baptist-supported colleges. When Jerry, their second child, received a full scholarship from the university Peter had attended, they solicited the pastor's counsel. During the pastoral conversations that followed, Jack and Rosemary learned to identify the various ways in which the preservation of family traditions or the maintenance of continuity with their past had been more important for them than providing room for individual growth within their family. Moreover, they came to realize that their son Peter *Gardner* was the only one in the entire extended family to be named after great-grandfather Gardner Griffin and that

Peter's commitment to spend a year living with the poor reflected the adventuresome spirit of Gardner more than all their subsequent preoccupation with the purity of the Griffin tradition.

CONTINUITY AND FAMILY STABILITY

The family mediates between the inevitability of change and the human need for continuity. Change is disorderly. If the family is to remain stable in the midst of change, some continuity is necessary. That stability, however, is for the purpose of providing a context in which change might occur. Because the Griffins had made continuity an end in itself, even ordinary change was difficult. Continuity is necessary for stability but it should not be achieved at the expense of the freedom of individuals within a family to maximize their own unique gifts.

There are several ways by which families seek stability through continuity. The recollection of stories and legends is often a useful way of helping to preserve the family's self-understanding. For example, the stories of the heroic deeds of great-grandfather Gardner Griffin had been told and retold in order to support the Baptist family tradition. And yet, until Peter's disruptive change, the Griffins had lost the principal value that the tradition preserved—a willingness to risk. Even when values are no longer consciously shared by the entire family, the legends that embody those values can remain a focus for the family's self-understanding. It is sometimes difficult for individuals in a family that is well defined by its mythology to feel free to change. Helping families understand the power of the myths they live by can, without disrupting the stabilizing continuity of those myths, create more freedom for change.

Name giving is another means by which a family seeks stability through continuity. While it is undoubtedly true that parents have a wide variety of reasons for naming their children as they do, one of the most common reasons is to insure continuity in the family tradition. It is often easy to trace a line of continuity in a family genealogy by noting a particular name that carries a blessing or an expectation. Sometimes a child is named for a beloved or deceased relative with the unconscious expectation that the child will carry on the valued attributes of that special person. From an early age I was told by my parents that I had been named after one of my mother's favorite brothers who died at an early age in a tragic farm accident. The natural closeness between mother and child was intensified by that association of names. We need to be alert to the emotional power of name giving to shape an individual's future while at the same time providing stabilizing continuity for the family system.

The preservation of treasured objects and family heirlooms provides another occasion for continuity. These can serve as focal points for family remembering. They are bearers of an inheritance from the past by which the family seeks to maintain continuity with its future. Saving the family farm or preserving grandmother's rocker can serve the interests of continuity.

Keeping family heirlooms, however, may also impede growth or change by cluttering a living space, or foreclosing vocational options, or limiting one's freedom to change. A friend of mine once broke a bowl that was a family treasure. Whenever his mother asks about the bowl, he feels compelled to spin another web in the deceit that shapes their relationship—and even colors his interaction with his present family. At forty-three, he is perpetuating patterns of family interaction in ways that suggest that the preservation of continuity is a higher value than honesty.

The most subtle form of continuity in the interests of stability is the inclination of any system to seek and maintain equilibrium. The family, like any human system, is a conservative institution. It seeks to establish and maintain homeostasis. Sometimes the need for homeostasis becomes an end in itself. The family will resist change in order literally to stay in the "same place." Children will ignore medical attention in order to take turns being sick and staying home from school in order to take care of their mother. A husband may develop physical symptoms that would subvert his wife's professional development. A wife may sabotage her husband's effort toward sobriety because she is reciprocally dependent on his drinking behavior. A family's unwillingness to deal with buried grief may evolve into a fixed equilibrium that prevents people from leaving home because "this family has already had enough heartache." In circumstances of this sort the family is stuck; its energies are devoted to restoring and keeping a fixed balance, even at considerable cost to individuals within the family.

If, however, homeostasis can be understood in a dynamic way, as something that is always changing as surely as members within the family change, then it creates a context that is both stable and open. There is always a delicate balance between openness to change on the one hand and on the other hand that continuity which is necessary to insure within the family system a stability sufficient for that change to occur. When a family is in trouble, it hopes to draw helping persons into its web of interactions in a way that will minimize change. Pastors' ability to help families depends on their escaping these webs. Pastoral interventions, which are sometimes designed to upset a dysfunctional homeostasis, are grounded in the conviction that change—and not continuity—is the enduring stability in the family.

SOCIALIZATION AND THE TRANSMISSION OF VALUES

Prior to the industrial revolution the family was generally regarded as the primary agency of socialization. It was described as the schoolhouse for society or the laboratory for social living. It was in the home that primary education occurred, religious belief was nourished, and people were taught the laboring skills that would enable them to contribute to the larger society.

Since industrialization, other agencies in society have been granted power to continue the process of socialization. Christopher Lasch has identified this new departure with the phrase "the socialization of reproduction."[1] Churches, schools, voluntary clubs, work guilds, television—all influence the process of socialization as much or more than does the family. The family is now only one unit among many that have the responsibility of preparing the young for living in society.

Despite the decline of its influence, the family still has socialization as one of its tasks—simply because the family generally provides individuals with their first experience of community. One of the ways in which the family functions to stabilize society is that of socializing the young. The family is where we are first schooled in the art of group living. Here we learn about sharing and responsibility. We internalize rules and roles that are necessary to sustain community life. We learn patterns of communication and interaction that are recapitulated in other social groupings. It is in the family that an individual is first controlled, restrained, and directed toward community's needs.

The family's efforts toward socialization are complicated by the pluralism that characterizes modern societies. Our modern celebration of diversity creates new tensions for the family. For example, a simple correspondence between a family's moral standards and those of the surrounding society cannot be assumed. Nor can the family avoid exposure to the moral confusion prevailing in the larger society. Parents often feel powerless in the face of peer pressure and the growing pluralism of values. Without the support of a common system of values and institutions that provide meaning and undergird personal significance, the family as an institution is often overwhelmed by the weight of a moral and spiritual load that it simply cannot bear alone.

As one response to the pluralism of values, families have sometimes closed themselves off to the world around them. The environment becomes the enemy. The family is perceived to be under attack from evil forces invading the home through radio or TV or the educational system, forces that promote dissatisfaction with traditional values. This perception of the environment as enemy has prompted some parents to organize efforts to homogenize society's values according to their own standards. They appoint themselves guarantors of the common good. They crusade against the "evil" outside the family and attempt to protect the family by keeping tight control over what their children see and hear. Socialization then becomes a narrowing enterprise that, by enhancing prejudice, diminishes rather than enhances social stability.

For the family the long-term consequences of such an approach to today's diversity of values are dismal. A family that has no vital interaction with its environment is likely to be consumed by stagnation. A new homogenization of values by family fiat is neither likely nor desirable anyway. The world in which we live is too richly diverse for all families to be stamped with the same mold. Moreover, the assumption—by individual or family—that one can locate evil "outside" is theologically unsound.

There is, however, an alternative to the creation of a closed family system as protection against cultural and moral pluralism, and that is to recognize that learning to decide among competing values is both possible and beneficial. It is an essential component of the socialization that occurs in family and church. Making choices in a pluralistic society is a difficult task. It requires both an understood system of values and the skill of decision making. The church's task in the face of pluralism is to help parents be clear and consistent about their values in order that they can provide their children with a platform to develop values that will be their own. Children also need opportunity to practice making choices as a part of the socialization process. One of the painful risks of parental love is that of allowing children, within a supportive context, ever-increasing freedom to make their own choices among competing values. It is equally important that the church provide a context of understanding for parents whose children reject the parental value system.

This approach to socialization depends on families being confident of their competence.[2] It also requires an openness to the environment. If a family becomes isolated and self-protecting, preoccupied with its own survival in the midst of a seemingly alien and hostile world, it is likely to teach its children to be responsive to and responsible for a very narrow circle. Though we do need the close emotional bonds of the family as a context in which to learn about love and sacrifice, there is always a danger that by expecting us to love some people more than others the family will in effect teach selfishness. Although I do not regard the family as inherently selfish, the radical claims of discipleship compel followers of Christ to look beyond narrow family ties.

The growing isolation of the family presents a serious obstacle to the fulfillment of its socializing responsibility. By developing an insular attitude that shuts out its environment, a closed family ignores its duty to society and becomes an end in itself. The family can be successful in modifying human self-centeredness only as it remains open to ever-expanding human communities and to the creation as a whole.

THE FAMILY AND A STABLE SOCIETY

The family is still regarded by many as the principal unit responsible for providing a stable social order. Proponents of this position argue that whatever strengthens the family strengthens society and that the reality of the world is sustained through the kind of conversation with significant others that is most likely to occur within the family. The modern nuclear family is the locale for acquiring the qualities and values that are necessary for the preservation of a free democracy. As such, the family might be called the seat of civic virtue, the linchpin of society, the nucleus of civilization. Because the family is the most potent moral, intellectual, and political cell in the body politic, the health and well-being of the family are regarded as critical for society's survival.[3]

There is truth in this position, but it can also be overstated. The family may indeed be a locus for conversation serious enough to sustain reality. However, the relation of the family to the larger society is more complicated today than is implied by the assumption that the family as a unit is capable of stabilizing society. Moreover, the socialization of production and reproduction has irrevocably altered the family's primacy as *the* constitutive unit in society. The family is a social linchpin more in memory than in fact. At the same time that its influence and size have diminished, social turbulence has increased. To expect the family to be *the* anchor for society is unrealistic.

Instead, the family has become a refuge *from* society rather than a fundamental unit *in* the social order. In today's world of impersonal bureaucratic organization, where production and rational relationships are the order of the day, it is understandable that the family is expected to be the center for human affections and emotional loyalty. The family is the place, after all, where we know that we belong, where we do not need a number in order to be recognized. We hope that the family will be a comfort station that provides a buffer against a complex and impersonal world. As a result, we have come to expect more and more from fewer and fewer people.

It is doubtful that the family can survive exclusively as an emotional refuge, especially when everybody is looking to receive solace and nurture. The privatization of the family can only lead to an emotional incest that is self-destructive. The family cannot survive unless it has a reason for being that transcends privatization and comfortable isolation.

What is required for the family's vitality is an ecological perspective that acknowledges an interdependence between the family and the larger society. The family's openness to ever-expanding communities is an anticipation of the eschatological vision in which all things potentiate and toward which creation moves in ever-expanding ways. The family's relationship to the environment is marked by mutuality rather than domination. The obligations of discipleship in God's realm continually push families of Christians to look beyond themselves.

THE FAMILY AS AN OPEN SYSTEM:
A THEOLOGICAL MANDATE

It may be said that one can measure the health of the family by the way it welcomes strangers. That is a concrete way of identifying openness as a necessary characteristic of a family's structure and function. Openness that fosters reciprocity between the family and its environment, an openness that encourages services to the larger society, is necessary for the survival of the family. This vision of openness is also fundamental to what we have called the family's second purpose—that of providing stability for the larger society in which it participates. Families best fulfill this function when they are open to the people and ideas within their environments. The family's ecology moves outward in ever-widening environments to include the neighborhood, the church, the particular society, and the entire human community. The principle of openness is the prelude to the interdependence that governs the family's interaction with these larger networks.

The family must be an open system if it is to foster in its young a sense of moral obligation to these larger human communities. The privatization of the family, which is intended to be protective, ultimately leads to moral bankruptcy. One can say therefore that in a sense a family "sins" by being closed. It violates God's intention of an open and interdependent creation. Being a closed system is contrary to the eschatological vision in which finite systems are open to God's new creations.

Creation is an open system in which God's creative activity continues to be that of making something new. In contrast to the traditional picture of creation as a closed system, perfect in itself and self-contained, Jürgen Moltmann has suggested that "if creation is subject to change and is open to time from the beginning, then it cannot be a closed system; it must be an open one."[4] The recognition that creation is an open system requires a shift from traditional patterns of dominance and subjection. The relationship between human and nonhuman systems becomes one of interdependence and mutuality rather than domination and exploitation.

This emphasis on openness to interdependence has implications for the church's understanding of the family and public policy. The relationship between the family and society has become a matter for public policy. Many social agencies interact with the family. It is necessary to make explicit how procedures and expectations from the public sphere will affect the family. Although public policy cannot enforce the openness necessary for a vital interaction between the family and its environment, neither should it impede such interdependence.

In the process of developing an explicit public consensus about the family, it is critical that the church be a clear and knowledgeable participant lest the state, by default, become the guarantor of the family in the public sector. If that process is governed by the rubric of interdependence, neither the church nor the government is the primary protector of family sanctity. The family, like the church and state, is accountable to God for the exercise of its purposes in creation. And yet all three social institutions interrelate in the care of humankind. They are interdependent means by which God continues creating and preserving the world. None has dominance over the other. It is theologically inappropriate for the family to isolate itself from interaction with the other institutions responsible for human care.

The church's contribution to the family-policy debate should be to insist on this interdependent model in which both church and state interact with the family in the care of people. Such a social policy for the family, a policy that recognizes the need for interdependence, will avoid governmental dominance, family isolation, and theological intransigence. By itself, the family cannot guarantee social stability. Only by establishing clear boundaries and interactional patterns between these three agencies in creation can God's continuing care be enhanced. We turn next to a consideration of interdependence as a theological motif for an understanding of the relationship between the family and its environment.

CHAPTER 4

Interdependence—
A Sign of God's Care

CREATION: ECOSYSTEMS AND HUMAN SYSTEMS

It is obvious even to the most casual observer that all of creation exists in a delicate balance. Advances in science have enabled us to see more and more precisely how all parts of the universe are linked together in a system of mutual influence. Teilhard de Chardin has observed that "the farther and more deeply we penetrate into matter, by means of increasingly powerful methods, the more we are confounded by the interdependence of its parts."[1] Everything is related to everything else. As in chapter 2 we spoke about change as the first of three characteristics of family structure, so here we speak of the interdependence of all living things as the second motif from creation that illuminates a theology for the family.

Like adaptability to change, the commitment to interdependence is essential both for the family as an organism in the world and for each particular family unit. Families that ignore interdependence in order to limit change do so at their own peril. All human systems, like the human creature itself, are interdependent organisms set within a network of physical, social, spiritual, and cultural relations. The family as a human system, like the whole of creation, is an ecosystem interrelated in a wonderfully mysterious and complex way.

The idea that human beings can stand outside of creation and dominate it represents a misunderstanding of interdependence. It is, however, the ideological base upon which industrialization is built, and modernization has simply exaggerated that notion of distance. The isolation of the modern family, like the present ecological crisis, is in part a consequence of this disregard of the interdependence of humankind and creation.

The belief that all of creation is a complex ecosystem changes our assumptions about human stewardship. The human, the animal, and the vegetative all mingle together and are fed by the same Creator. In an interdependent creation there is no justification for domination. All things belong to God. The interdependence of all creation is undergirded by the God whose sovereignty is safety and whose care is always creative.[2]

In his essay *Creation* Claus Westermann insists that the creation narratives of the Bible do not separate humankind from the whole of creation. Moreover, the relationship between man and woman, which mirrors the interdependence of all things, is primarily characterized by mutuality: "To mutual help must belong mutual understanding in word and response, in silence and activity. The community of man and woman in our present day can also be described in this way, despite all differences and changes in culture."[3] This mutuality of human community is echoed in the following verses from Ecclesiastes:

> Two are better than one, because they have a good reward for their toil. For if they fall, one will lift up his fellow; but woe to him who is alone when he falls and has not another to lift him up. Again, if two lie together, they are warm; but how can one be warm alone? And though a man might prevail against one who is alone, two will withstand him.
> (4:9–12)

Our inclination to deny interdependence is one manifestation of sin. Subjugation and stinginess and isolationism are responses of fear that violate human community by denying mutuality. Because the human creature has both the capacity and inclination to disregard the necessities of creation, interdependence needs to be a fundamental characteristic of family structure in order to compel people in families to do the good that they may not always want to do.

THE FAMILY AS AN
INTERDEPENDENT SYSTEM

What is necessary for the ecosystem as a whole is also necessary for each particular family. The family as a human system is made up of individuals who are related to one another interdependently. It is an interlocking puzzle in which a change in one affects the whole. Individuals in a family have distinguishable roles, and their interaction of those roles is governed by rules. The mysterious power of attachment that prompts people to seek and to belong to one another is fulfilled within the context of an organism in which mutuality and interdependence are the norm.

In order for the parts of a system to work together interdependently there needs to be clear separation between each part. Interdependence within a family, therefore, requires autonomy as well as mutuality. At the same time, an interdependent family structure with clear but permeable boundaries allows and encourages individual units to be autonomous. Boundaries function to protect the differentiation of each individual within a family system. Boundaries are also essential in order to preserve the particular subsystems within the larger family web or to distinguish the tasks and responsibilities of the parental unit from the sibling unit.[4] Boundaries between the parts of a family need to be both clear and permeable in order to insure respect of identifiable parts and accessibility of those parts to one another.

Families may err either in terms of too many or too few boundaries. If the boundaries are too rigidly held, the resulting pattern is one of disengagement and exaggerated individuality. Because of this skewed sense of autonomy, the mutuality necessary for effective family functioning seldom obtains. People in the family tend to interact with one another from behind barricaded space, protecting privacy and independence at all costs.

The absence of clear boundaries leads to emotional fusion in which the individual parts or members of a family are indistinguishable. In such an enmeshed or close-binding family, it is difficult to have distinct feelings and ideas because togetherness is understood in terms of sameness. Individuality is stifled by exaggerated togetherness. In both extremes, interdependence is limited.

The family as a system is a community made up of individuals whose personal worth and autonomy are protected by that community. At the beginning of life, each human being needs to be regarded as an endangered species needing protection. The family is a sanctuary for the protection and nurture of human life in all its particularity. For that reason, clear but permeable boundaries are not only essential to the interdependent functioning of the family as a system; they are also essential for the maintenance and development of an individuated self.

SIN IN THE FAMILY

Where the family is concerned, sin may occur in two fundamental ways. Selfishness continues to be one manifestation of sin. In the family it can take the form of exaggerated independence. Selfishness not only rejects the mutuality necessary for community; it denies the sacredness of human particularity and inhibits spontaneous giving and fellowship. The failure to claim one's distinctiveness, however, is also sin. Unclear boundaries and excessive togetherness end in self-negation and deification of the family. Thus a family may sin by caring too much or by caring too little. Inadequate individuation, which is the consequence of too much togetherness, is as sinful as faulty socialization, which generally results from overly rigid boundaries and excessive independence.

The distinction that feminist theologians have made between sin as self-deification and sin as self-negation is at the heart of the family's struggle for interdependence as a balance between autonomy and mutuality. Self-justification, alienation, and dominating self-assertion are images of sin that are common to disengaged families that limit interdependence by means of rigid and impermeable boundaries. Triviality, distractibility, diffusiveness, lack of an organizing center, and dependence on others for self-definition are sins of self-negation common to families in which the boundaries are not clear enough to nurture particularity.[5]

BALANCED INTERDEPENDENCE

Maintaining the balance between the primacy of the individual and the primacy of the community, between autonomy and mutuality (the balance that is necessary for interdependence), requires a willingness to accommodate. Development of the distinctive gifts that God has given to each family member cannot happen unless all are willing to sacrifice or modify their individual expectations for the sake of others and the system as a whole. Such sacrifice is a matter of justice. Otherwise a family system may function at the expense of the member who is expected to do all of the accommodating. Genuine interdependence requires equal accommodation. Equal opportunity to develop one's gifts is possible only when everyone has an equal responsibility for practicing accommodation.

Families are also able to function interdependently if the alliances within the system can shift and loyalties are not absolutized. If one relationship in a family demands exclusive loyalty at the expense of other relationships, the resultant family equilibrium precludes interdependence because at least one person is regularly excluded. Boundaries within a family system must be permeable in order to maximize the possibility that the separate individuals and units within the family can connect and interact with one another in ways that promote both autonomy and mutuality. Such interaction is sustained by at least three distinct human expressions of the need for connectedness within community—complementarity, intimacy, and covenant.

Complementarity

Frederick Buechner in his book *Godric* describes how complementarity is a part of friendship: "Human folk love one another for the way they fill each other's emptiness. I [Godric] needed Mouse for his strength and mirth and daring. Mouse needed me for my mettle and wit."[6] Every human relationship of complementarity is an acknowledgement that no human being is a self-contained unit.

Complementarity at the beginning of a marriage generally involves a delicate balance of needs met. It is a kind of altruism that, when needs are reciprocally met, helps to create and sustain the marital bond. Even when individual expectations are kept secret, when needs are so deeply buried that neither partner is aware of them until they are unmet, marriage partners often look to one another to fill in the empty spaces. Someone who is reticent and shy may marry someone more gregarious and social. Someone from a family that majored in togetherness may seek someone from a less closely knit family in the hope of finding some breathing room. Someone who is creative but chaotic may look to a marriage partner to bring order out of chaos. The reason why opposites attract is that the whole is greater than the sum of its parts. Complementarity is one kind of interdependence.

Although complementarity is a recognition of human interdependence, it may also mark the kind of excessive dependence that inappropriately limits individual maturation. Complementarity may be reason to marry, but not reason enough to sustain a relationship in which growth occurs. Complementarity may even add a burdensome weight to a relationship. No individual within a family can or should have to do everything. Moreover, we need to be cautious about allowing the strengths of others to prevent the fostering of our own strengths. Complementarity becomes a problem if the needs that the other is to fulfill are excessive. Complementarity is easier in marriage if people have already learned to be alone.

Because people change it is not easy to maintain the balance of reciprocal needs met. It is important that people preparing for marriage be helped to make explicit the expectations they have of their marital partner, how they expect the other will fill in their own empty spaces. It is equally important that marriage partners in counseling begin to ask how the initial complementarity has been modified in their case to accommodate the individual changes that have occurred. When it is said that people in a certain marriage seem to have outgrown one another, this is generally because they have been unable to adjust the original complementarity of their relationship to meet changing needs and growing strengths.

Intimacy

The family's capacity for intimacy is what makes possible the balance between autonomy and mutuality that we have identified as the hallmark of interdependence. It is easier to be truly separate within a family when one can count on warmth and caring to keep people together. At the same time, people are not likely to risk being close unless they have the freedom to be separate and distinct individuals within the intimate community. Respect for the particularity of another is what makes genuine intimacy possible.[7]

Intimacy presupposes identity. Being intimate is possible only if there is an "I" who is both the subject and the object of the interaction. The infant/parent dyad begins as a relationship of affection that is necessary for human survival and ordinarily becomes a relationship of intimacy as the child's identity develops. Some families, however, may remain affectionate but never become intimate because of the limits that are set on becoming separate persons. Without clear boundaries, affection becomes absorption rather than intimacy. Without permeable boundaries, the distance that intimate relationships require becomes isolation. Genuine intimacy is possible only in those families that have learned how to be together separately.

Intimacy within the family presupposes distance. Boundaries within a family make it possible for each individual or subunit in the system to develop an identity and carry out individual functions without undue interference from others. In the emotional sphere, setting others at a distance makes it possible to share a doubt or sorrow or joy within the family without fear of being swallowed up by the system. The commitment to participate with one another insures that the emotion will not be ignored. Clear but permeable boundaries make intimacy possible by protecting the differences within a family system without prohibiting significant interacting.

This recognition that difference is necessary for intimacy makes it mandatory that families develop a constructive response to conflict. The most positive way of managing conflict, while also enhancing the possibility of its resolution, is to prevent other family members from being drawn into the conflict. In troubled families it is likely that a conflict in any part of the system will involve the whole system. Families will endure conflict only if they can contain it and thereby insure the possibility of reconciliation.

Physical intimacy is a central part of family life. People are prompted to marry because they find physical intimacy with a particular person satisfying. Although a satisfactory sexual relationship is certainly not the only thing that keeps people together, a marriage would be difficult to sustain without it. Within the bonds of marriage, and given the mutual respect of a marital relationship, there is freedom to explore and celebrate erotic love as a dimension of physical intimacy.

From the beginning of life the relationship between parents and children is sustained and nourished by physical intimacy. The relationship between an infant and the nurturing one is both physically intimate and pleasurable. The pleasure that a woman experiences while nursing is a biological encouragement for mothers to provide the intimate nurture infants need. Touch is a necessary dimension of nurture in early life. As children grow older, it is increasingly necessary to recognize the boundaries to physical intimacy within a family. Incest and other forms of sexual abuse are a violation of the physical and emotional boundaries that normally make emotional intimacy one variant of family interdependence.

Human beings are by nature communal. Our attachments are not restricted to physical dependency and needs for survival. We are community-oriented creatures. Human beings need to be connected to others in order to survive emotionally. Attachment is a fundamental human impulse. We are free therefore to promote autonomy and individual uniqueness without any fear that it will lead inexorably to rampant self-centeredness. And yet it would seem that the promotion of autonomy and equality for women as well as men has made intimacy in the family harder rather than easier. If, however, intimacy presupposes autonomy, we now have the possibility for a deeper level of mutuality in the family.

Covenant

The interdependence that is inherent in all creation is finally sustained by humankind through intentional commitment or covenant. It is true that we do not choose the family into which we are born. Children often speak of it as a gross injustice that we are located in a particular family without even being consulted. *That* we are born and *where* we are born is beyond our choice. However, our choice to marry and remain in a family as a lifelong commitment is an intentional act. A marriage may not endure, a family may become dysfunctional, if the persons involved are not committed to one another with a matching intensity.

Covenant, even more than commitment, is an apt metaphor for understanding interdependence within the family because it assumes a relationship of mutuality. Walter Breuggemann has suggested that in the context of the biblical faith the family is generally understood in covenantal terms. All human relationships are covenantal when "they are a) based on vows, b) open to renegotiation, c) concerned with mutual decisions, d) affecting all parties involved, e) addressing life and death issues, and f) open to various internal and external sanctions."[8] Within the covenant, subordination is precluded. The family as covenant is a community in which husbands and wives, parents and children honor one another by treating each other with seriousness.

The family is a covenantal relationship in which the interdependence of each member is a source of both pain and joy. The family is rooted in creation and shaped by human history, always forming and being reformed as family members take each other seriously and acknowledge the needs, demands, and gifts that shape human life together. Regarding the family in terms of covenant does not diminish either change or diversity. But because people in families are always changing, the family must be constantly renewing its covenant.

The ability to make and keep interpersonal covenants is not only fundamental to humanness; it is essential for maintaining interdependence within the family. The family as covenant is born not out of need but out of commitment. Understanding the family in terms of covenant also maintains a balance between the extremes of individualism and collectivism in the larger community, society, or state. If the purpose of the family is understood in terms of individuation, the image of covenant is a hedge against excessive self-centeredness or a preoccupation with family privacy.

The family cannot exist apart from interdependence with its environments. It cannot be solely a refuge, because it is an agency of God's initiative for the sake of creation and for the sake of generations. Moreover, willingness to covenant transcends the complementarity of needs and attachments that naturally bond God's creatures together. Covenanting is an intentional act which nonetheless acknowledges that humankind shares interdependence with all creation.

CHAPTER 5

The Family
and
Individuation

The first two purposes we have identified—in chapters 1 and 3—relate the family directly to communities and environments beyond itself. The family is the agency in creation that is responsible for the continuance of the human species. The first purpose of the family, the procreative purpose, thus obligates the family to the whole of creation. It is also the whole human community that benefits from the exercise of responsible limits to procreation. The family needs to maintain a positive perspective on the future lest it disregard its creative responsibility to that larger human community in favor of its own more personal objectives. Participating in the procreative process through the family is an intentional act that serves God's creative purpose on behalf of human continuity.

The second purpose of the family, the purpose of social stability, is related to a particular social order. The family enhances stability within a particular society by effectively socializing its young through an openness to its environments that in turn fosters interdependence. Privatization of the family runs counter to this purpose and represents a deviation from the vision of creation and of all structures within the creation as being open to God's newness.

Procreation and social stability are thus the first two purposes of the family. The family fulfills both purposes when it functions as an open system that looks beyond itself to ever-widening circles of human responsibility and creative interaction.

The family exists, however, not just for the sake of the larger social structures and environments, but also for the sake of the individual. The process of self-definition, of claiming one's own unique personhood, is called individuation. Individuation occurs within the context of the family because it is here that each individual is first named as a distinct and unique creature and here that the individual is provided with the basic nurture needed for physical well-being and overall growth.

LEARNING HOW TO BE
SEPARATE TOGETHER

I have identified individuation as the third and primary purpose of the family in order to maintain a balance between the community and the individual. The goal of the individuation process is to enable people to be separate together. Being separate selves who are capable of being together with other separate selves is necessary for a vital society that both celebrates diversity and honors community. This third purpose of the family is primary only in the sense that individuation, even more than socialization or procreation, is uniquely a family responsibility. The shaping of human particularity has its beginnings in the context of the family.

The phrase "being separate together" is intended to convey the equal importance of both community and individual. It is not possible to be an individual except in relation to community. Commitment to community need not exclude freedom to be one's self. And the vitality of any community is enhanced by the participation of individual selves. The conflict between the individual and the family is often more perceived than real. Being together is as natural as being separate.

This image of being separate together corresponds to Tillich's categories of individualization and participation. For Tillich both individualization and participation are ontological categories; they are qualities of everything that exists. In its fullest form, Tillich describes being separate together in terms of persons in communion—one individuated self, participating with another completely centered self: "The person as the fully developed individual self is impossible without other fully developed selves. . . . Persons can grow only in the communion of personal encounter. Individualization and participation are interdependent on all levels of being."[1] Being separate together, therefore, is not something added to human life; it is something essential for life in communities and families.

Being in a family means walking a tightrope between individuating and participating, between separating and coming together. To be separate together means that personal distinctiveness and selfhood are preserved in family interaction. Being separate together has as its goal autonomous individuals who are committed to participation in the family and in larger social units in order to create new settings in which individual growth might continue to flourish. Although the structure and purpose of the family in relation to the larger society has changed and will continue to change, the family remains the primary locus of individuation.

The process of individuation leads to self-definition rather than self-deification. It has to do with developing autonomy, becoming free to differ, valuing one's worth, and claiming the validity of thoughts, feelings, wishes, and fantasies because they are one's own. It means that one's body is one's own—to cherish, nourish, and use responsibly. Being individuated is a prerequisite for interdependence, which in turn is essential for human community. Autonomy and community-mindedness are the interrelated goals of individuation and socialization.

Becoming a separate person capable of participation with others is ordinarily a lifelong task. The physical severing of the umbilical cord that once united the mother and her newborn is a paradigm for that ongoing emotional process of separation. As we grow up, our physical survival depends less and less on our parents. We learn more and more to walk, cross the street, talk, go to school, and take care of ourselves. If, however, we continue to depend on our parents for self-definition and self-esteem, the process of individuation is impeded. If we spend time and energy seeking our parents' approval, living up to their expectations, worrying about whether to them our feelings are acceptable or our decisions right, we may reach physical maturity well socialized and eager to accommodate others, but still not be individuated. On the other hand, we may grow up rejecting—in the interests of freedom—all the values of our childhood and still not be individuated. People who run away from home seldom "leave home." One can be oversocialized or undersocialized and still not be free to be oneself.

Some families make the process of becoming separate persons difficult; others make it easy. Some families are more concerned about ensuring proper socialization than about nurturing human

particularity. To put it another way, some families major in separateness, while for others togetherness is the norm. Every family is
somewhere on a continuum between exaggerating individuality on
the one hand and demanding uninterrupted togetherness on the
other.

Families in which individuality is highly prized often appear dis-
connected. In these families that promote separateness, freedom to
do your own thing is more important than being in community. Such
families, however, interfere with individuation in a surprising way.
Becoming a distinct person is an empty process if there is not a
significant emotional attachment from which to separate.

Personhood presupposes community. This means that to become
a separate individual one must first be connected with others. And at
the same time, the possibility of community presupposes being separate. There is no intimacy without identity. Separateness and togetherness are organically interrelated. The family provides the
communal setting for growth in particularity, which in turn fosters
interdependence.

BAPTISM, FAMILY, AND AUTONOMY

The question of autonomy is central for the family's purpose; it is
also at the heart of all struggle for human dignity. Human particularity is difficult to maintain in a society that has become faceless and
bureaucratic. As a response to the complexity and coldness of modern life the privatization of the family is counterproductive because
it magnifies human powerlessness and isolates the family from any
significant interaction in society.

The family needs to be a place in which people are encouraged to
discover their own particular gifts. Parents love their children best
by encouraging the development of autonomy and by allowing them
to come into their full potentialities as separate persons who are
committed to being together with other separate persons. Society is
served best by individuals who can speak and act autonomously, and
hence responsibly, with one another. The family does not exist for its
own sake but in order to be the context in which people are individuated for service in the world for Christ's sake. In that sense, a
Christian theology for the family is a celebration of human agency.

The baptism or dedication of infants contributes to the development of human autonomy. To be baptized means at one and the

same time to be chosen and named by God as a distinct individual *and* to be incorporated into a community that transcends all human particularity. We are called out of our families for service to the world. This understanding of the baptism of infants enhances the development of human autonomy because it is a reminder for parents that the child in their home is theirs and yet not theirs. We let our children go, because ultimately they belong to God. Baptism calls into question any impulse to hold onto our children. There is no place for close-binding families within the community of the baptized. Because our children belong to God, it is our responsibility to help them become separate and distinct beings who are nonetheless committed to participation in meaningful community.

Baptism is also a sign for the Christian that individual growth cannot be an end in itself. Baptism means initiation into a community that is shaped by the event of Christ, a community that draws its members into ever-larger communities. Baptism is an invitation to a struggle of dying and rising, of life and death. Baptism is the beginning of a discipleship that demands our ultimate loyalty. The magnificent promise of baptism is that God will not abandon us on the way.

The family is one context in which we are prepared for discipleship. It is that locus of criticism and care in which we discover the gifts that are ours to give and also develop the courage to use those gifts for the sake of others. Baptism is a reminder to parents to let their children go so that they might become autonomous enough to serve the world for Christ's sake. It is also a reminder to children, as they continue the lifelong process of leaving home, that the Christian story irrevocably draws us beyond the family into larger and larger communities of concern. Individuation is necessary for Christian vocation.

PASTORAL CARE OF FAMILIES AND THE INDIVIDUATING TASK

Leaving Home

Pastors will do well in their care and counseling to be mindful of the need for individuation. Three phenomena in the patterns of family response merit special attention in this connection.

The process of leaving home is often as painful as it is necessary.

Simply put, it involves the separation of generations. For people in families, it means the loss of a dependable relationship, a comfortable place, a familiar face. For parents, the fundamental task is to act out the conviction that loving means letting go. The parental love that lets go and sets children free to serve in the world parallels the love of God in Christ. For Christian parents, baptism has been a sign from the beginning that our children already belong to God.

For children, leaving home is complicated both by their parents' unwillingness to let go and by their own reluctance to leave. For young people whose family of origin has provided a safe refuge from the world, it is a frightening prospect to leave home. If a family is particularly close-binding, leaving home may be perceived as an act of disloyalty; children are led to believe that the stability of the family depends on their staying home. In most circumstances, leaving home physically is a natural though painful event in the lifelong process of individuation.[2]

Leaving home may precipitate emotional crisis not only because it challenges loyalties and threatens safety, but also because it represents an assault on childhood patterns of dependency and on parental omnipotence. Because the world outside the family seems complex and bewildering, there are those who opt for the safety of home rather than risk dismantling their childhood myths about the world. In the Western world the process of leaving home is complicated by the absence of social structures for separating parents and adolescents, by protracted educational programs that extend the period of adolescence, and by the emergence of an affluence that middle-class children cannot expect to achieve and enjoy when they do leave home.

The lifelong process of leaving home is marked by significant moments along the way. These moments include early experiences of being separated from parents for a period of time, speaking up to parents, choosing to side with one's marital partner in a family dispute, buying a different make and model of car than the one father drives, switching political parties or religious affiliation, or moving to Wyoming. Until both parents have died and we are finally orphans we are in a sense always leaving home. It is important for both children and parents to understand that we leave home so that we can go home again. How children leave—and how parents let them go—will affect how easy it will be to return.

Pastoral interventions with people in families often occur when there is trouble in the individuating process. Children who think differently may be treated by their family in ways that diminish rather than enhance self-esteem. Pastors are often called upon to straighten out "thinking that has become too different." Teen-agers who run away from home often spend a lifetime running away from home. The freedom they seek eludes them because they are still bound emotionally to the home from which they run. It is a difficult pastoral task to explain to the distraught parents of a runaway child that, however destructive and disruptive, this may have been the only way their child believed he or she could ever leave home. Young people who think they have severed all ties with their family by marrying someone unacceptable to the family often end up in the pastor's office unhappily married—and still emotionally dependent on that family. It is enormously important that pastors give both theological and pastoral clarity to the conviction that loving means letting go.

Scapegoating

The phenomenon of scapegoating represents another way in which individuation can be disrupted in the family. Scapegoating refers to the process by which one member of a family is identified as the family's "problem." The family as a system seeks to maintain equilibrium and avoid change by blaming a hyperactive child or a delinquent adolescent for all the family's trouble. The sins of the family are heaped upon the one member who perpetuates the system by bearing its sins. Sometimes the family unconsciously elects one of its members to be individually sick in order to divert attention from the family's sickness. The family is convinced that it has neither time nor energy to address larger family matters because they must attend to the one who bears the family's sickness.

In either variant of the scapegoating dynamic the effect is the same—the well-being of one individual is sacrificed for the sake of the whole. The individuation of the family scapegoat is arrested in order to be sure that he or she does not outgrow the assigned role. The process by which an individual is designated to play the scapegoating role involves a confluence of family needs and individual predilection.

Giving real help to scapegoating families is an arduous and delicate task because families often find it difficult to relinquish their own diagnosis. Blame for the family's discomfort must be located somewhere. It is not enough to say that the family is troubled; our sense of linear causality presses us to insist that a particular individual is the source of the problem. It is unlikely that the family will accept a more systemic definition of the problem until they are convinced that their own original diagnosis has been accepted by the helping person. The task of redefining the problem in terms of the family as a whole requires interpretative skills and the gentle exercise of pastoral authority. In chapter 8 we will consider further this process of redefinition or reframing.

Accommodation

The third pattern whereby individuation is disrupted for the sake of the whole is that of accommodation, often identified with the role of the woman in the family. Although accommodating is not restricted to women, one long-standing assumption has been that a woman's natural bent is to set aside her own needs for the sake of the larger community. We have all heard magnificent stories about women who went without a new dress for twenty years in order that their children might have proper clothes. Autobiographies are replete with stories about women who set aside small amounts from the grocery money in order to pay for a son's viola lessons or buy a daughter's new dress for her first dance. Sacrifice, we have been led to believe, is a particularly feminine virtue.

It is indeed a remarkable virtue to be able repeatedly to set aside one's own needs for the sake of those you love. Untold numbers of people have risen to positions of greatness because of self-sacrificing wives and mothers. Because this pattern is so pervasive and long-standing, it is not surprising that the current movement toward women's liberation is frequently regarded as one of the social factors putting stress on today's family. As more and more women have decided to abandon the role of primary accommodator within the family and to claim their own gifts and abilities, the tensions between personal development and family belonging have increased.

Vital balance within the family depends on the willingness of each member to accommodate and compromise for the sake of the whole.[3] This process requires a willingness to express desires and needs clearly, even when they cannot all be granted. Every member also has an equal responsibility to adjust to the claims of others in the family. If only one person does all the accommodating, no one else learns how to go about it. Recent changes in the roles of women in both family and society now make it possible and necessary for men and children too to practice the art of accommodation. The question is finally one of mutuality and justice.

Learning the art of accommodation, which presupposes a prior capacity to claim the validity of one's own needs and wants, is a necessary part of individuation within community. Accommodation by everyone involved is an absolutely essential ingredient for a vital family life. It is surely a manifestation of corporate sin if the family depends on only one person to be the primary accommodator. The just family is one in which the needs and wants of all are considered and attended to in an appropriately mutual manner.

SUMMARY

Our pastoral interventions need to acknowledge the dynamic balance between leaving and joining that is essential for the survival of the family. This dialectic can be stated in a variety of ways. Becoming separate means that you were once connected. At the same time, the possibility of community presupposes being separate individuals. One must disconnect in order to reconnect. Personhood presupposes community. Identity precedes belonging. Being in a family involves a delicate balance between individuating and participating, between separating and coming together. Becoming a separate self can occur only in the context of communities that love and let go. The central purpose for the family in our society is to find ways for each of us to be separate together.

From the perspective of the Christian tradition, the family's structure can be more diverse than its purposes. There have been and will continue to be a wide variety of structures in which the purposes of procreation, social stability, and individuation may be realized. For the sake of the wider human community, and for the sake of individuals within families, these three purposes may be regarded as normative. Although each purpose is consistent with an understanding of creation as the arena in which God continues to effect care, each purpose is also relativized by the demands of discipleship in

God's realm. Even individuation is not an end in itself but is pursued for the sake of the world. The obligations of Christian discipleship transcend the many social and individual needs that the family fulfills. The family is simply a context in which we discover and nurture our gifts for the world in such a way that we can then also give them away.

CHAPTER 6

Diversity—A Sign of God's Extravagance

The promotion of individuation in family, church, and society will inevitably lead to greater diversity. Plants, fish, planets, rocks, germs, and viruses all testify to the diversity of creation. The differences between a walrus and a hummingbird, a rhinoceros and a raccoon, are evidence that the Creator has an appreciation for variety and a notable sense of humor. The diversity of nature is a sign of the extravagance of God's creative love.

The diversity that is readily apparent in both nonhuman and human organisms is also characteristic of the structure of the family. A theology for the family that takes creation seriously will lead to the celebration of diversity in the structures of the family as well as in the world around us.

Throughout history and across cultures, and even within particular societies, the family has been and continues to be shaped in a wide variety of ways. Families have been matrilineal as well as patrilineal, polygamous as well as monogamous, hierarchical as well as egalitarian, matriarchal as well as patriarchal, single-parent as well as multi-parent, extended as well as nuclear. Such diversity of family structure is not just an accommodation to necessity; it is a consequence of physical, social, and psychological changes that are built into the process of human growth toward maturity. The varying circumstances in which people live require a pluralism of family form in order that individuals might have an appropriate context for care and growth.

Diversity is not always regarded as a self-evident sign of God's generosity. Sometimes it is regarded as dangerous—as promoting disunity or generating conflict. The inability to tolerate diversity leads to prejudice, isolationism, and self-protection based on fear.

Tension and conflict are fundamental and inevitable consequences of diversity, and prejudice is the most perverse method for managing the conflicts it produces. Prejudice is fueled by the conviction that whatever differs from what I regard as the norm is dangerous and should be eliminated. The length of hair, the kind of music that is played, the clothes that are worn, the books that are read, the ideas that are held—all may become occasions for conflict in any human community, including the family.

Some families choose to dissolve conflict by maintaining that differentness is an illusion: What may appear to be a difference in family structure or a difference of opinion within a family is in fact only the outward manifestation of a single underlying view. Such an approach simplifies family life and provides a reprieve from the moral and emotional demands of living with difference, but frequently it does so at the expense of individual growth and truth.

Another way of skirting the complexities of diversity is to maintain that the way things were at the beginning is normative. Human institutions like the family are, or at least ought to be, as God created them initially. Evolution, change, and adaptation are all regarded with suspicion because they seem to undercut the stability that God ordained from the beginning. From this perspective the family as institution will best be restored by reestablishing an earlier and more divinely ordered form. Within a particular family, healing may necessitate the return to an earlier state or stage that time and nostalgia have invested with unwarranted authority. In both instances, the mystery of change and the wonder of diversity are reduced to uniform images that alone bear the stamp of God.

CELEBRATING DIVERSITY

There is a biblical view that stands in sharp contrast to all of these efforts at diminishing the diversity of creation. Praise for the wonder and variety of God's creation is a dominant theme in the Psalms. The beauty of all things living provides the psalmist ample material for meditating on the magnificence of the power and wisdom of Yahweh. Here the majesty and diversity of God's creative work is cause for celebration. All creatures "great and small" express in ways "beyond counting" the glory of the Lord (cf. Ps. 104:24–26).

Recently we have acknowledged the delicate balance between

unity and diversity among the early Christians. Even though all things were united in Jesus Christ, there was room for a pluralism of life styles, vocations, and spiritualities. Paul's image of the body as a single organism whose various parts exercise different functions is more than simply an illustration; it is itself a miracle of creation. Oneness is not diminished but enhanced by individual differences. The unity of human community is the consequence of a positive interpretation of originality and individuality.[1] Within the Christian community individuals are able to help one another precisely because they are unlike each other. Diversity is part of the miracle of creation. It is a gift of God.

In a quasi-autobiographical book entitled *Celebration of Life* Rene Dubos has similarly suggested that diversity is necessary for creativity, even though it is also the genesis of inefficiency and conflict. Without diversity human beings are not fully free to be creative because they do not have sufficient options from which to choose. "While great diversity in any situation increases the complexity and numbers of problems, it also generates original and enriching solutions for the very problems it creates."[2] So, for example, living with family diversity may be more difficult but it enhances human potential by expanding the sphere of the possible; in that sense diversity is a requirement for survival of individuals and the family.

Even while we are here emphasizing the creative potential of diversity, however, it is also necessary to recognize its limits. The Christian doctrine of creation embodies a moderate rather than an unlimited pluralism. Too much uniformity can inhibit growth and stymie creative energies, but too much difference can disintegrate communities like the family. There are limits to the diversity that any system can endure. There are also individual psychological limits to diversity and change. No one is infinitely flexible, even though we are all more capable of tolerating diversity than we realize. To impose unnecessary limits on God's richly variegated creation, however, is to reject the Creator's generosity.

DIVERSITY AND THE DEFINITION DILEMMA

The theological and political task of defining the family is complicated by the emerging pluralism of family structures. Because of competing definitions of the family, it is both difficult and essential to maintain a delicate balance between diversity and constancy. Until recently, despite differences of structure or form, one assumed that the nuclear family consisted of parents and children who lived together. This traditional picture has been radically altered, however, by the frequency of divorce and remarriage in modern societies. Although the family today may still follow the older formula, it is no longer obvious just whose parents or whose children are living in which particular household: his, hers, and ours may also include theirs. The proliferation of parents in the nuclear family has also magnified, and thereby complicated, the extended family. What a family looks like today is no longer as self-evident as it may have been in times past.

There are voices today that contend that to limit the definition of family simply to parents and children is not sufficient to account for present diversity; people who marry without any intention of having children also constitute a family. For others seeking to define the family, kinship alone seems too restrictive. In order to take into account the broad spectrum of relationships that label themselves family, some of which do not follow traditional kinship patterns, it has been suggested that family ought to be defined according to function rather than structure or some preordained set of relationships. Protection, shared income, increased social opportunities, and emotional support are also regarded as criteria for recognizing familylike arrangements.

The dilemma of defining the family has been further complicated by the widespread use of "family" as a metaphor for describing a variety of human communities. The worshiping congregation may in some respects indeed resemble a family, but it is not a family. The popular "family of God" metaphor for Christian community has only limited usefulness. At best, it may provide useful clues to the complexity of congregational life, which often includes dynamics that resemble sibling rivalry or family feuds as well as the comfortable warmth of being known and loved. At its worst, use of the family metaphor may diminish the dialectic between the necessities of creation and the demands of discipleship that is characteristic of the Christian life. Neither the family nor the church can be a haven from the world. We need to be circumspect in our use of the term "family" in order to preserve its usefulness as a metaphor referring to those human communities that are in fact bound together by kinship.

For our present purposes, therefore, the family is here defined as a kinship system of two or more persons which involves a commitment to one another over time. Kinship is achieved by marriage, birth, or adoption. Because family structure is linked to family purpose, it is necessary that the family be defined in such a way that its purposes of procreation, social stability, and individuation might be fulfilled. Nonetheless, a definition of the family should allow enough flexibility for a variety of structural forms and patterns. The focus on kinship limits that variety according to the purposes of the family. The term "household," however, which also has strong biblical roots, may provide a useful metaphor for designating nonkinship communities.

Our emphasis on kinship here is not wholly arbitrary. It is grounded in the theological conviction that being in a family, like being born, is finally not a matter of human choice but the result of God's activity. The family is a social unit made up of both willed and unwilled connections whose reality lies entirely outside our inclination and whose inescapability is absolute.

We can rail against the family or reject it, but we cannot escape from it. At a fundamental level, children never fully leave home. Nor, at an emotional level, is divorce possible for those who have once bonded themselves to one another. We cannot fully take apart what God has put together. The usefulness of "family" as a metaphor depends on our retaining some element of this powerful inescapability.

The family is also the place where God places us at birth. To say that God places us in a family is parallel to suggesting that babies have to have someplace to go when they leave the hospital. We are not just anywhere. We are placed into a specific family in the world. That placement is not a matter of our choosing. The family is where God first locates human beings in creation. Belonging to a family is an extension of God's continuing creational care.

THE SOURCES OF DIVERSITY

Throughout this development of a theology for the family I have more than once suggested that the characteristics necessary for the family's interaction with the larger environment are equally necessary for the effective functioning of each particular family. Interdependence and adaptability to change are essential for the functioning of families. The same is true of diversity. Although some families work hard to stamp out differentness in favor of an artificial unity enforced by uniformity, families that function well have learned to tolerate and even to celebrate diversity in their midst, honoring the particularity of each family member.

Learning to live with diversity is an intensely important issue for a world in which pluralism is becoming an increasingly local matter. The family can be a laboratory for learning tolerance only if it is a context in which differentness is allowed. Diversity in the family has at least four sources—one's family of origin, gender, individual development, and the human life cycle.

Family of Origin

Each individual brings to the process of forming a family a particular set of values, interactional patterns, established customs, and role expectations from his or her family of origin. Sometimes the differences between the two sets may be insignificant or easily negotiated. In other instances the differences are too great to be easily compromised or even tolerated. For example, the celebration of holidays is an emotionally charged issue that is negotiable as long as loyalty to one's family is not linked with maintaining a particular tradition or custom. My wife's family opened presents on Christmas Day, while in my family of origin the tradition was to open them on Christmas Eve. We compromised and now open the presents on Christmas Day while retaining the traditional Swedish meal on Christmas Eve. Even such a simple compromise was not easily achieved. That small change took some time and required a respect for the validity of each tradition and a freedom to change without being disloyal to one's family roots.

Different customs or patterns of behavior often mask deeper and more substantial values. Food preparation, child-rearing practices, bedtime rituals, and religious ceremonies often carry a weight of obligation to one's family traditions. When those traditions are reinforced by ethnic identity or class values, the conflict over differentness is intensified by larger loyalties. In caring for families, it is both difficult and essential for pastors and counselors to help people identify the genesis of an emotion that is generated by differences established in the families of origin.

The development of a way of managing diversity in the family begins already with the process of getting married. Helping to make explicit the valued traditions derived from each family of origin is part of the task for pastors working with couples preparing for marriage. Each partner needs also to identify those differences from the other family of origin that are deemed least acceptable. Learning how to negotiate through differences to a position of tolerance or even celebration is one of the important early tasks in marriage.

Gender

A second source of diversity within the family is gender. It has long been assumed that the differences in roles and interactional patterns within the family were largely determined by sexual differences: Women were not only biological mothers; they were by nature the primary nurturers of children. Men were less involved with child rearing except when their strength was required for the exercise of discipline. Women were more dependent but also more dependable; it was their responsibility to keep the family together, make the hearth a home, and be ready to satisfy their husband's emotional and sexual needs. Men headed the household; they were responsible for the family's well-being but were not always dependable. The gender-specific differences within a family were presumably preserved by unspoken but reasonably clear-cut rules.

These diversities in the family that were previously thought to be generated by gender have now been complicated even further by the realization that such roles and interactional patterns are in fact not gender-specific. It is simply not the case that men act one way and women another solely because of biological differences. Anatomy is not destiny. In single-parent families, women are in fact heads of households and men are primary nurturers. In an emotional sense, it is quite possible that mothers can be fathers and fathers can be mothers. Thus to gender diversity within the family has been added the dimension of unpredictability.

When Bill and Kathleen were married each of them assumed reasonably traditional roles that were gender-specific. Bill took out the garbage, wrote the checks, mowed the lawn, and serviced the car; he helped with the dishes and cleaned the toilet too but only under protest. Kathleen did the cooking, sewed her own clothes, painted the kitchen cabinets, and organized their social lives. These traditional patterns continued for a time after the children were born. When the youngest child entered first grade, however, Kathleen decided to return to school herself. Shortly after that, as a part of her education, she had to be away from the family for two months. She thrived in the highly competitive, complex world of business management. While she was away the children were delighted to find their father pressing pinafores in the laundry room. But Bill was unsettled by the newfound pleasure he had discovered in his shifting roles. He sought help from his pastor when he suddenly became aware that after putting the children to bed he was happily paging through cookbooks rather than reading legal briefs.

Bill and Kathleen's family illustrates two things: (1) the family, as a system, is generally able to assimilate change better than the individuals within it. For individuals within a family, questions of self-identity are sometimes linked to changes in male and female behavior; (2) as long as the boundaries are clear and the communication straightforward, families do not require gender-specific behavior in order to be stable. Adapting to changes in traditional marital roles requires both personal and systemic adjustment that we may find difficult to do alone. The existence of support groups for men and women experiencing role changes is an important form of ministry to people in families today.

The diversity of the family must be tempered by what is ideal and by what is real. Two parents who love one another are better than one. That is ideal. However, children can grow to responsible maturity if they are cared for by at least one adult who loves them enough to let them go. That is real. The diversity of the family is also affected by the physiological equipment we have inherited from our past. Diversity of membership, role changes within the family, and environments altered by technological developments that require different family patterns are all tempered by the fact that Westernized human beings "are still genetically equipped only with an ancient mammalian private heritage that evolved largely through adaptations appropriate to much earlier times."[3] For the changes that have been made in modern family life it is sometimes cumbersome that males do not lactate and that females must bear children.

While biology does not and cannot ever have the last word, a theology for the family, if it is to be rooted in creation, cannot ignore anatomy. Alice Rossi is correct: "A society more attuned to the natural environment, in touch with and respectful of the rhythm of our body processes, will ask how we can have a balanced life with commitment both to achievement in work and intimate involvement with other human beings."[4] Men and women do experience the world differently, whatever the genesis of that difference. Fathers and mothers respond differently to their offspring. The family is inescapably linked to the biological processes through which God continues to care for creation. Until we can be clear as to what is biology and what is socialization, it is important that we honor the differences between men and women in the family, yet without insisting that all spouses and parents fit into traditional gender-specific roles.

Individual Development

Even if it could be established that all men and all women think and act in ways that are predictably different and determined by gender, there would still be diversity in the family because each individual is unique. From the beginning of life each individual brings to the world his or her own uniqueness. It is the responsibility of the family to respect the particularity of each child from the moment of birth. One aspect of care involves attending to that uniqueness. The family is the context in which each individual is encouraged to discover and actualize his or her own gifts for the world. Such an approach to the family is supported by the conviction that the God who numbers the hairs on our head honors our particularity, and hence delights in diversity. Our love for one another in the family should do no less.

One of the purposes of a family is to foster individual growth. The goal of this individuation is a differentiated self that is capable of autonomous feelings, thoughts, and actions but at the same time committed to participation with other selves in community. The family that fosters individuation for each of its members needs to be prepared for the possibility of diversity. That diversity is always moderated by the community's need for order and unity. Each family will establish and maintain its own balance between unity and diversity.

The Human Life Cycle

The fourth source of diversity is related to gender particularity and individuation but is worthy of separate mention. The family is composed of individuals who are at different stages of the human life cycle. Therefore parents and children are working at different and sometimes conflicting developmental tasks. The developmental task of middle age, which includes coming to terms with finitude and the necessity of limits, is not easily compatible with the adolescent's need to decide among seemingly unlimited options. Young adults who want to establish themselves in a career may not have either the time or the energy to attend to the nurturing needs of young children just beginning to find their way in the world.

Everyone in the family needs freedom to attend to developmentally appropriate tasks. Accommodation and compromise are essential in order to insure that within the family all members have the support needed for their particular life-cycle agenda.

SUMMARY

Pluralism of family structure is an extension of the diversity that is inherent in the creation which God has labeled good. Families, like people, fish, flowers, and snowflakes, are wonderfully and frightfully different. Where the family is concerned, there is no one design that has exclusive divine approval. The celebration of diversity in all of life is a faithful way of responding to God's creative extravagance.

Change and diversity are common features of all human environments. The family is no exception. Because creation is an open system that is continually changing, all human beings and human structures participate in the still open, uncompleted process of creation. We celebrate diversity not because differentness is easy to accept but because it exists for the sake of freedom and creativity. The family, as part of the unfinished creation, is always becoming something new. Hence, there is no one way for families to be. The family is always changing.

Diversity of structure is one consequence of this continually unfolding creative process. Diversity is a necessary dimension of each family that honors individual particularity. Our pastoral response will require an ability to help people, in the midst of contemporary pluralism, to find ways of forming a family that are consistent with the Christian tradition and at the same time responsive to the needs of people in industrial societies. For this task, the modern diversity of structure is a sign of God's extravagant care that is always creating anew.

The family as a human structure is a part of creation. In developing a theology for the family I have suggested three themes that are signs of God's intention for creation—the tolerance or even celebration of diversity, the adaptability to change, and the commitment to live interdependently in the world. Each of these themes not only characterizes the relationship between the family and the larger society but also identifies dynamics within each family that help it to fulfill its purpose.

What is necessary from the perspective of creation, however, is relativized by the obligations of discipleship. In God's realm the family is affirmed, but its significance is also limited. Our theology for the family and our pastoral work with families are shaped by this dialectic.

PART TWO

THE PASTORAL CARE
OF FAMILIES

CHAPTER 7

Effective
Family Functioning

A systems approach to the care of families begins with a normative vision of family life. The family, we have seen, is a human system that maintains simultaneous commitment to the individual and to the community as a whole. We have already examined the three major purposes of the family—procreation, social stability, and individuation. For the sake of discipleship in an increasingly complex world, individuation must, of the three, be regarded as primary because it is so essential for Christian vocation.

Change, interdependence, and diversity, we have also suggested, are three characteristics from creation that are necessary for family structure if the family is to be open to what God is making new. Because people change, the family always changes. Like the whole of creation, the family as a human system is a delicate balance of interdependent parts. The diversity of the parts is essential for its unity as a functioning organism. Any of these three characteristics can become a structural issue for the troubled family. Work with a troubled family is enhanced by attention to these structural issues.

In addition to family purpose and structure, there are three dynamics essential for effective family functioning—flexible roles, adaptable rules, and dependable rituals. Each is essential for the functioning of a family, and yet each is relativized by the promises of the Christian gospel. Although from the Christian perspective we are not defined by family roles, or redeemed by family rules, or sustained by family rituals, all three of these dynamics are normative and necessary for effective family functioning.

ROLES

A family is composed of interdependent members. Each member has assigned roles. These roles define an individual's place within the system and help to shape the family's structure. Roles in the family are related to biological functioning, status within the system, and the expression of emotions. Families function best when there is flexibility about the sociobiological roles, clarity about the structural roles, and equality with respect to the emotional roles.

Flexible Sociobiological Roles

The process of joining a marriage inaugurates a role shift that takes longer and is more traumatic than is usually realized. This role shift actually helps to make possible the emotional bond of marriage. If an individual is reluctant to give up loyalty to the role of son or daughter, the achievement of marital commitment will be postponed. It is true that when a son becomes a husband or a daughter becomes a wife neither gives up completely the former role status. But the very process of leaving home implies a beginning in the shift away from the primacy given to that earlier role.

The roles of husband and wife were once relatively clear and gender-specific: A husband was someone who was the primary wage earner, took out the garbage after two reminders, initiated sex, handled the finances, and walked the dog—but never learned how to boil water. A wife was someone who did volunteer work at the church, cooked the meals, responded in sex, spent too much money, gossiped over tea, and cleaned up after the dog—but certainly would not know how to fix a plugged sink.

While we continue to use the role labels of "husband" and "wife," the content of these roles is no longer predictable. Couples who wish to divide the marital roles and household tasks not according to sex but according to convenience or talent will require clear communication and willing negotiation. Where roles are not absolutely defined, such things as too little margarine, no baby sitter, overdrawn checkbooks, or an empty gas tank can generate conflict. There is less conflict among couples who either hold to traditional roles for men and women or else reject those traditions altogether, than there is among couples who disagree on what husbands and wives should do.

Attention to the marital roles is an important component of a counselor's premarital work. Couples can be helped to understand how roles were apportioned in their families of origin—as a way of initiating a consideration of their own division of marital roles. Even when we self-consciously decide on marital role patterns different from those of our parents, our parents' role modeling remains powerfully significant in our lives. Pastors who visit regularly with a couple early in the marriage will be able both to observe and to foster development of the marital relationship through repeated consideration of role adjustment.

In an effort to maintain systemic equilibrium, a family may resist the role changes that must inevitably accompany other changes in its life situation. In order to establish the family as a context for individuation, there needs to be maximum freedom for individuals to discover marital roles that fit. At the same time, the freedom needed for individuation must be accompanied by an accommodation to roles for the sake of the whole system.

Assuming the role of parent creates a whole new set of challenges and crises. Biological fathers and mothers do not automatically become parents. Nor are the parenting roles of father and mother biologically set. As long as the roles in marriage and family were traditionally drawn, it was relatively clear what mothering was and who did it. The same was true of fathering. It was believed that the social roles of father and mother were determined by biology. Fathers were distant and instrumental, while mothers were warm and expressive. Given that pattern it is not surprising that the father often was and is the family outsider.

There are biological factors that shape what is learned and the ease with which the sexes learn certain things about parenting. The fact that women bear and give birth to children cannot be disregarded in defining parental roles. Nor do men have the biological equipment necessary for nurture at the beginning of life. Men do not derive from nursing that physiological pleasure which is designed to insure that such nurturing will continue; for example, holding a bottle at 4 A.M. provides no intrinsic pleasure. "If a society wishes to create shared parental roles, it must either accept the high probability that the mother-infant relationship will continue to have greater emotional depth than the father-infant relationship, or institutionalize the means for providing men with compensatory exposure and training in infant and child care in order to close the gap produced by the physiological experience of pregnancy, birth, and nursing."[1] Although the sociobiological roles of parenting should continue to be redefined in the direction of greater freedom and flexibility for men and women, we must also steadfastly recognize the biological factors that shape what we learn. All perspectives on parenting must, in some fundamental sense, be biosocial.

Pastoral interventions with couples around the birth, baptism, or dedication of a child offer natural opportunities for being alert to any current difficulties the family may have in making role changes. The loss of a spouse by divorce or death while children are still living at home offers another occasion when people may be helped to reexamine parental roles. Whether or not the mother and father roles are both embodied by only one person, it is necessary that the parental role always include both closeness and distance.

Clear Structural Roles

One purpose for maintaining boundaries within a family is to insure proper differentiation between parents and children. We belong to only one generation at a time. Keeping the distance between the executive or parental system and the sibling system is essential both for family stability and for effective individuation. Families are likely to become troubled if parental authority is not clearly executed. That is not to say that all authority in a family resides with the parents. Nor does it imply that the way to save families is to reinstate rigid parental authority. What is most important is that parental roles be clearly defined and consistently executed. Where there is clarity about parental roles, however, and permeable boundaries exist between the executive and sibling subsystems, the family is likely to function well and children will be free to be children.

Clarity in structural roles might be disrupted in a variety of ways. One or both parents may be unwilling to accept the obligations of the father or mother role because they prefer being a son or daughter, or they resent the intrusion of children upon the marital bond. Sometimes one parent has usurped exclusive parenting responsibility, letting the other remain distant. Sometimes one parent abdicates all responsibility for parenting, preferring instead simply to play with the children. In such circumstances, or when because of death or divorce there is actually a one-parent family, one of the children may be elevated to the executive system as the "parental child."

The parental child is one who has been granted the privileges and responsibilities of a parent, a child who is included in the confidences of the parent in ways that the other children are not. In every family, authority may be temporarily given to one of the children, but clearly that authority is derivative and will be recalled by the parents when the circumstances change. If, however, with tacit parental approval a child assumes that authority permanently, the result is role confusion as well as unclarity of boundaries in the system. Generally such role confusion is related to disrupted communication between the parents and diffused decision making in the family. The parental child may have his or her individuation abbreviated by the premature assignment of adult responsibility.

> When Dorothy was a child, she had been required to care for her younger siblings and her invalid father so that her mother could support the family. Dorothy married at an early age, partly as a way out of those family responsibilities. When her marriage was terminated fifteen years later she returned to college and actively sought to fulfill a lost adolescence. In a poignant counseling session with her children shortly after the divorce, Dorothy revealed the extent to which she had turned over parental authority to her thirteen-year-old daughter while longing wistfully herself, in a manner appropriate to an adolescent, for the world outside. Dorothy was determined at long last to claim her own freedom from responsibility, even though it meant that her daughter would have to repeat Dorothy's own adolescent experience of being a parental child.

The clarification of boundaries between parents and children is a central part of pastoral work with families. Where there is conflict between parents, one child may be drawn into a position of inappropriate authority as peacemaker or rescuer. This task of clarifying the parental role is particularly crucial for helpers working with single-parent families. Pastors or counselors who were the parental child in their own family of origin need to be cautious about assuming too much surrogate responsibility in their efforts to promote family stability. The pastor needs to be able to offer assistance to parents in their executive tasks without being drawn into the system in ways that undermine necessary parental authority.

Equality in Emotional Roles

The family as a system is also maintained by roles that are more emotional than biosocial or structural. Emotional roles are those patterns of behavior that accomplish the expressive tasks of the family. If the family is an organism with a life of its own, then it is appropriate to speak of the family as such being sad or troubled or happy. Sometimes particular individuals within a family are designated to express one or more of these emotions. Other emotional roles are often more instrumental than expressive; members are expected to organize the family's activity with a view to enhanced enjoyment or orderliness or virtue. All members of the family need an equal share in the distribution of significant emotional roles.

Although some emotional tasks seem to be common to all families, many emotional roles are peculiar to the particular system. Moreover, these emotional roles are not sex- or gender-specific, nor are they necessarily limited to one person in the system. Roles are assigned by the family in order to foster interaction and to maintain the emotional balance of the system. For example, families need a camp director who will organize picnics or visits to Grandma or summer holidays. Families need someone to bear pain or stop fights or make mischief. Larger families need a historian to keep the record straight and a switchboard operator to make sure proper connections are made. The family scapegoat (discussed in chapter 5) is a negative emotional role, but one that a family may nonetheless perceive to be necessary for keeping the system as a whole in balance.

Family emotional roles are generally assigned with the individual's concurrence. Even one who has been selected as the family's scapegoat usually complies in some way with that selection. Because systems theory understands causality in a circular way, however, it seems both impossible and unnecessary for us to determine which came first—systemic selection or individual concurrence. The determination of family emotional roles involves a combination of both systemic needs and individual proclivity. Not everyone can be the family clown or the family healer. Because individual proclivity contributes to emotional role selection in the family, equality of distribution has some limits.

There are four emotional roles that are frequently distributed within a family system: (1) being right, (2) being the bearer of righteousness, (3) doing wrong, and (4) being bad. In traditional marriages, not unlike the caricature in the television series about Archie and Edith Bunker, these emotional roles were often distributed in the following gender-specific way:

Traditional Marriage

Husband	Right	Bad
Wife	Righteous	Wrong

In this pattern, husbands were usually right ("Father knows best") but a little bad ("After all, men will be men"), while wives were the bearers of goodness and righteousness ("Her children rise up and call her blessed" [Prov. 31:28]) but basically wrong ("She thinks like a woman"). Although the rigid assignment of these roles was personally destructive, it provided a balance of power in the system. Part of the current upheaval in family life results from the disintegration of that traditional gender-specific alignment of emotional roles in the family.

While some emotional roles can remain relatively fixed without harm either to the family or to individuals within it, these four emotional roles at least must be rotated equally if each family member is to develop his or her gifts for service in the world. It is a matter of justice in the family. Being wrong and being bad are inescapable, but families often become troubled when these roles are unchangeably identified with particular individuals. If one child is the "bad seed" or another "cannot do anything right," the family system may be stable at the expense of the individuals within it. Positively, for the sake of the just distribution of self-esteem, everyone in a family needs to be right sometimes, and everyone needs to feel like a good person once in a while. People are likely to cling tenaciously to righteousness as a way of maintaining power in the system.

A Doll's House Marriage

Torvald	Righteous	Right
Nora	Bad	Wrong

Henrik Ibsen's *A Doll's House* portrays a devastating variable of this quadrant of emotional roles. Nora is finally judged as both wrong and bad by her husband Torvald, who assumes for himself both virtue and truth. What Nora thought she was doing as a gesture of love and kindness to her husband becomes the occasion for her banishment from the household as both wrong and bad. In his own commentary on the play, Ibsen suggests that Nora eventually loses all sense of right and wrong. Her natural feelings on the one side and her belief in authority on the other lead her to utter distraction. With this quadrant, as with all other emotional roles in the family, it is essential for the well-being of both the individuals and the system that each emotional role be available to everyone.

Summary

Roles are necessary for family functioning. Human systems cannot function without clearly identified roles. Our roles, however, do not define our value. Roles can never be more important than the individuals who fulfill them. Freedom from being defined, even by roles that are necessary for the system, is guaranteed by the gospel promise that God's love transcends what human institutions require. Each family member has received gifts that are to be discovered and nourished within the family with a view to that individual's service in the world for Christ's sake. Our family may name us, but it is God who particularizes us in our baptism. Each of us is placed in a family and then called out of that multi-membered organism to be a unique child and partner of God.

RULES

The family has a life of its own. It is an organism made up of interacting and interdependent parts. These parts are identified according to assigned roles. The action of these parts, their role within the family system, is governed by rules that establish the norms of conduct and patterns of interaction within the family organization.

Family rules are both explicit and implicit. The rules about brushing teeth, going to bed, cleaning up, doing chores, spending money, and coming home are generally explicit. In rule-oriented families these explicit rules may be evoked regularly in order to exercise power or settle disputes. Other family rules—about the expression of emotions, behavior in the world outside the family, bringing home odd ideas and people—may be equally clear but never spoken.

These implicit rules are the most powerful. Precisely because they are implicit they are not negotiable. Implicit rules are evoked in a family only after they have been transgressed.

Rules are necessary in order to govern any human system. Within the family, rules regulate the proper use of authority and the just distribution of roles. They are essential in order to clarify boundaries, enhance communication, and facilitate change. Family rules work best when they are flexible, explicit, and unambiguous. Families are likely to become troubled when the rules are rigid, when they are unspoken but assumed, and when they embody double-binding messages. Often the task of the helping person is to make hidden rules explicit. The absolute power of hidden rules can usually be diminished only by breaking them.

Flexible Rules

Because people and systems change, rules that govern a system such as the family need to be flexible. Bedtime rules invariably change as children grow older. Managing the comings and goings of adolescents requires less dexterity but more adaptability than putting a four-year-old to bed. A family rule about being home for the evening meal may need to be replaced by a rule that requires advance notification regarding who is eating when. Rules about cleaning one's room may be replaced by new rules about shutting the bedroom door. Although these few illustrations are drawn from the world of children's rules, the same principles apply also to adult rules. Children quickly learn in matters involving family interaction to disregard rules that the parents themselves disobey. It is difficult, for instance, to insist that children never interrupt a conversation or speaker when the parents themselves are always doing precisely that.

Flexibility in family rules does not mean that families should have no standards. Every human community is organized around shared values that establish coherence and order interaction. Because of the pluralism of values in our society today, one can no longer count on an easy harmony between social ideals and family rules. For this reason one must pick one's absolutes carefully. Parents should be clear about which values and rules they regard as essential.

In order to insure that rule flexibility obtains within the family, everybody must learn the art of compromise. The process begins with parents who can settle their differences about family rules without choosing up sides within the family. Effective parenting may best be described as the art of selective accommodation. It is necessary of course that parents be clear about the values they wish to transmit to their children. But rigid rules are counterproductive for effective family functioning since they do not allow for growth and change. Indeed rigid rules often mean a basic disregard of individual growth and of change for the family as a whole. Rigid family rules often substitute uniformity for loyalty. They may fix family interaction at a particular juncture in the family's history; changes that have occurred beyond that favored time are simply ignored or repressed because they disrupt the stability of the system. Rigid rules are generally designed to maintain systemic equilibrium and to prevent change. Recognizing the place of change in creation and in the family means that rules need to be flexible.[2]

Implicit and Explicit Rules

The rules that usually have the most power in a family are those that are implicit and hidden. They shape the family's behavior unwittingly. As long as family rules remain implicit, they cannot be criticized, debated, or negotiated. There is usually also a metarule that even forbids asking about the rules. As long as the rules remain implicit, family members have no way of challenging the authority figures who have the power to enforce them. Only after the fact does one learn that a family rule has even been broken.

Implicit family rules have many purposes. Sometimes they protect secrets known only to a few. Sometimes rules that are implicit limit diversity by rejecting, or more likely disregarding, anything new that comes into the family. Some rules, like many expectations in marriage, are kept hidden because of fear that they will be rejected as silly. Sometimes implicit rules are designed to limit individual growth by discouraging participation in any activity that might foster autonomy. Sometimes a family will seek to guarantee moderation by limiting the expression of certain emotions. One can often identify implicit rules simply by asking about which emotions were regarded as acceptable and which were unacceptable in one's family of origin.

Rules remain implicit in order that the people who hold the power may be able to keep it. Any change in hidden rules threatens the power of those who are the keepers of the rules. Keeping rules implicit is therefore one way of preserving the status quo in a family. The breach of a family rule often has the indirect effect of publicly identifying those who substantively have the power to make and keep the rules. It also poses a direct challenge to the hidden power center within the family. The helping person who wishes to expose and break implicit rules must therefore be prepared to exercise legitimate authority. It is usually possible to name a forbidden subject or ask an unacceptable question so long as the helping person is able to remain outside the emotional sphere of the family.

Pastors who regard themselves or are publicly regarded as upholders of the good may find it difficult to be naughty enough to break a family rule. But precisely because of their moral integrity, pastors are in the best position to help families discover that the family will not collapse if its rules are made explicit, or even broken. Such breaking of family rules, however, should be done with great care. Families that hold on most tightly to inflexible and implicit rules often live in fear that they will be shattered if a rule is transgressed. Helpers who work with families also need to be sure that each family discovers a new and more constructive source of stability to replace the loss of power that is experienced when an implicit rule is made explicit.

Unambiguous Rules

Families are often immobilized by a lack of clarity regarding family rules. Ambiguity as to family rules can keep everyone guessing about what to obey. Children are sometimes told not to do one thing, the assumption being that they will then know automatically that this means they are not to do something else as well. Lack of clarity, like hiddenness, is a mechanism for resisting change. As long as the rules are ambiguous, people are likely to keep things the same. Sometimes unclear rules unexpectedly obligate people. For instance, everyone in a family may agree to change vacation plans without realizing that this also obligates them to attend father's golf tournament.

The most powerful examples of ambiguous rules are those that involve the sending of a double-binding message. The recipient is then torn between two conflicting messages. To obey half the rule means that the other half must be disregarded or disobeyed. Such a double bind involves a distortion in family communication that confuses and eventually immobilizes. If a mother's words to her child are filled with warmth and invitations to intimacy while her nonverbal messages push the child away, she places the child in a double bind. The child cannot respond to the invitations to intimacy without violating the nonverbal signals about keeping distance.

It took me some time, for example, to figure out that my desire for my daughter to *want* to practice the piano created a double bind that actually made it harder for her to practice at all. My nonverbal message to her was that she ought to practice. My verbal message was that she should *want* to practice without my insisting. Because I wanted her to want to practice, I did not insist that she do so. Because she did not want to practice, she was in a double-bind. If she practiced without wanting to, she disobeyed the verbal message; if she did not practice at all, she disobeyed the nonverbal message. The only way out of that impasse was for me to become less ambiguous about my messages.

Breaking a family's pattern of sending double-binding messages is a complex therapeutic task. Pastoral intervention with double-binding families can occur naturally in a couple of ways. A pastor may help a family recognize the problem by reporting his or her own experience in being confused by the family's rules; this can be done gently by making clear that it is the pastor's own experiencing of the family that has led to the reported confusion. The family is then free, if it wishes, to disregard the observation as that of an outsider who does not understand. Second, in their own general pastoral work pastors can convey the message that unambiguous communication is a form of truth telling in human relationships. We may never know all the truth there is to know and tell, but in our communication with others we can be clear about what we do know, making sure that our "yea means yea" and "nay means nay."

Maxims as the Bearers of Family Rules

Because many of the rules that govern a family are implicit and hidden, people have difficulty identifying them. Encouraging people to recall family sayings or maxims, which are generally carriers of family rules and behavioral expectations, is one way to make them explicit. Both rules and maxims exist to support the myths around which a family organizes its self-understanding. A family myth is like an emotional coat of arms reflecting the principles or values that influence the way a family functions. Both family rules and family myths are likely to be less available for examination than maxims or sayings commonly repeated in the household. There is generally a consistency between maxims, rules, and myths that help the family as a system to hang together.

Not so long ago, my son identified a maxim that is central to our family's life. Walking out of a used bookshop laden with more books than we needed, we were complaining about spending too much money—at which point he jokingly recited a phrase that has been often repeated in our family: "We couldn't afford not to." Taking advantage of good bargains is not unlike seizing opportunities to enrich experience. The rule embedded in the maxim is that, whenever possible, we ought not to miss opportunities for enrichment. Therefore our first inclination is to say "yes" rather than "no" to most invitations. By following that maxim, of course, our family's time is often fuller than it should be, but the myth that we are a growing, stretching family is sustained. The impulses ordering our family's life are radically different from those of the family that insists: "If you can buy a sailboat for only ten cents but you don't need it, it's no bargain."

Eliciting family maxims is helpful in at least two ways: (1) it helps a family to make explicit the rules that actually have power; (2) it identifies divergent traditions that come into conflict at the formation of a new family. My maternal grandfather would often say: "You can laugh your way to hell but you can't laugh your way out." Though I do not remember the maxim being used in my family of origin, until it was told to me recently, and though the rules about levity in his family were largely implicit, the meaning of my grandfather's maxim continued: Making jokes and having fun are dangerous. The overwhelming seriousness that has constantly characterized my family was fostered also by another maxim that reflected the urgency of time, one that I often heard father repeat: "Too soon we grow old and too late smart." The rule carried by that maxim was that in a family which lives with the awareness of the temporality of all things one should not waste time, so even if levity is not all that dangerous it would nonetheless be a waste of time. The hidden rules embedded in such maxims have an ongoing influence, so making them explicit can ease the path of change.

There is a wide variety of maxims from which families can choose. Some reflect the value of hard work: "A winner never quits, and a quitter never wins." Others the value of frugality: "A penny saved is a penny earned." Or efficiency: "Don't go to the kitchen empty-handed." Some maxims promote high expectations in the family: "If you want to get something done well, do it yourself." Still other maxims prescribe interpersonal behavior: "If you can't say anything nice, don't say it at all," or: "The best way to get along is to be quiet." Some sayings promote family togetherness: "Just think, this is the last time we will all be together." Others diminish individual self-esteem: "You're not worth the salt that goes into the bread." Whether they are original with the particular family or borrowed from a more universal collection, such maxims usually reflect the unvoiced rules that prescribe behavior and govern the system in the interests of fulfilling its myth.

> Barry came from a family that lived by the maxim: "Schöne Leute haben schöne Sachen" ("Nice people have nice things"). Karen's family prized frugality ("Waste not, want not," her father would always say) and commonness ("You got to get the hay down where the sheep eat it," her grandfather had always said). The conflict between the two traditions became evident already in the planning of their wedding. Barry's extravagance and Karen's stinginess continued into the early part of the marriage and lingered as a point of contention in their relationship. The values they brought to marriage from their families of origin were couched in maxims not easily set aside.

Exploring maxims can be particularly helpful to pastors as they work with couples in the process of forming a new family. It is both enjoyable and beneficial to use maxims as a way of identifying the different rules that people bring to marriage from their own families of origin.

Summary

Families need rules in order to function effectively. Yet neither individuals nor families are saved by their obedience to rules. Families need clear structures and appropriate authority in order to create the context in which people can grow. But families are not preserved either by rigid rules or forceful parental discipline. Even flexible rules are not enough because all of us—people within families as well as people not in families—fail to be what God intended for us to be. Rules in the family do not eliminate sin. As a matter of fact, they may even make our sinfulness more apparent. Probably in no other context of human life does our sinfulness show as clearly as it does in the family. None of us can escape the recognition of our sinfulness by those who see our vulnerability most clearly—the other members of our family.

Living in a family should make us realistic. In this way the family continues to perform its responsibility for criticism as well as care. In family interaction tough love and tender love are blended together in ways that allow us to see ourselves as we are. It is sometimes a frightening truth that we are re-created in our own family members, especially our children. Marriages sometimes fall apart, and families become troubled because in the family we find out more about ourselves than we can bear. The family needs to be a context without pretense, in which we can openly confess our fault and then hear a forgiving word from those who know us best and love us most.

The recognition that our sinfulness is most evident in the family makes forgiveness an essential component of being children and parents together. It is the promise of forgiveness that transforms a rule-oriented system into a laboratory for living with grace. It is the practice of forgiveness within the family that overcomes resentment and deters conflict.

Because the family is a part of creation, that creation which is not all that God intended it to be, we are frequently disappointed and sometimes destroyed by our families. In any family there is often more criticism than care, more judgment than grace, more rancor than love. The incidence of family violence throughout human history is further evidence that evil exists inside as well as outside the family. Families are dangerous. At one level, our pastoral task may be to help individuals know just how the family works in order that they can protect themselves from harm. While I do not share David Cooper's uniformly gloomy judgment of the family as the enemy of autonomy,[3] I do believe that we need to have a realistic appraisal of the family as a flawed but necessary institution. Those who regard the family as a new source of salvation, or who see evil only in the world outside the family, or who find the family a useful metaphor to describe any nurturing relationship or context, are asking more of the family than it can possibly provide.

RITUALS

As a human system the family is composed of interdependent members, each of which has assigned roles. The action of these roles is governed by rules that establish the norms for conduct in the family. The interaction of these roles within the system generally occurs according to predictable patterns or rituals that provide continuity and stability for the family as a structure.

A ritual is an action, or series of actions, sometimes accompanied by formulae, that regulates transactional patterns within a family. A ritual may be overtly prescribed in terms of time, place, and participants; for example, in connection with a family reunion or birthday celebration it may be fully spelled out who is to come, what they are to bring, and how long they will stay. A ritual, however, may also be more covert: Family routines like putting children to bed or eating a meal usually evolve in a less explicit way.

A ritual is a symbolic process that unites or otherwise influences its participants so that they act in a way that is supportive of the organism as a whole. A ritual's first purpose is in relation to the system. It focuses the behavior of all participants in the direction of a common goal. If the goal is that of welcoming Father back home from his trip, that goal will determine what ritual is necessary and normative. Excessive noise or jumping on Father—otherwise unacceptable behavior within the family—may in this instance be an approved part of the ritual because it furthers the goal of welcoming. A ritual is a patterned transaction governed by a delicate feedback system in which each part triggers and monitors the behavior of every other part and all behavior is influenced by previous behavior. In the broad sense in which it is being used here ritual includes such interactional patterns as cultural customs, life-cycle rituals, and family traditions as well as daily routines.

Customs, Rites, Traditions

The preservation of particular ethnic or family customs increases diversity in the larger society while at the same time regularizing the life of a particular family. Cross-cultural studies of families reaffirm the need to recognize the validity of cultural customs in matters of mate selection, extended family involvement, and care of the aged. Although every society has seen family structure change in the direction of a more nearly universal uniformity, there is at the same time a growing recognition of the unique contribution each culture makes in the overall understanding of individual and family life. As the capacity to tolerate diversity increases, it seems likely that particular cultures will be encouraged to preserve their own ways of ritualizing significant events in the family's history.

The way a family navigates through difficult moments in its life cycle is frequently determined by external factors. Some life-cycle rituals are shaped by cultural custom; others reflect contemporary social patterning; still others are formed by the sacramental structures of a religious tradition that may also be culturally linked. Family traditions are more likely to be specific with respect to an extended family or clan. The transference of these traditions provides stability and continuity from generation to generation. Such traditions are a sign of identification for families, and sometimes a test of loyalty in the process of leaving home. Every new family is forged out of emotionally charged traditions relating to birthday celebrations, Sunday meals, entertaining guests, the raising of children, or the giving of gifts. For this reason it is necessary that premarital work by pastors help to foster an awareness of the power and validity of family traditions so that the process of negotiation about traditions may be initiated.

Cultural customs, life-cycle rituals, and family traditions all seek to keep a balance between continuity and change. Because they generally transcend the particular family, they also link each family with a larger human community. We keep traditions alive in order to maintain continuity with our own history; without traditions and family customs, it is difficult to connect with one's past. When traditions become paramount, however, there is increased likelihood that the system will remain closed to its environment and to change as well. People do not serve traditions; for the family, as for any human community, traditions exist to serve people.[4]

Family Routines

The rituals that most frequently influence a family's interaction are those daily routines that are idiosyncratic to each family. At the beginning of any marriage, the couple usually accomplishes certain delicate tasks related to the setting up of a household by establishing specific routines. Spouses develop routines for going to bed and getting up from bed, for setting and clearing the table, for making and drinking coffee, for being naked and having sex, for sharing the bathroom and the morning paper, for selecting programs and watching television, for prayer and worship. These routines will be influenced by patterns from each one's family of origin as well as by habits acquired on one's own. It takes time and a willingness to accommodate in order for couples to develop routines that will insure both private space and mutual accessibility within their marriage. The process is often complicated by their differing needs and expectations with respect to privacy and accessibility. Such development of routines, however, is an essential part of their task in developing and fostering intimacy.

The addition of children to the family often disrupts many of the routines a couple has previously established. Sleeping routines are altered to accommodate nocturnal rendezvous with hungry infants. Cleaning up the children may preempt the routine of clearing the table. Routines for leaving and coming home become more elaborate because more people need to be guaranteed accessibility to one another. It is no longer possible for Alice just to kiss Martin before going to work because there are also Jennifer and Michelle, and Per, each of whom wants at least two kisses. The capacity to develop new routines that take into account changes in the family will make it possible for the system to keep connected despite the growing autonomy of its members.

Bedtime rituals are frequently good indicators of a family's ability to adapt to the changes that occur as children and parents grow older. The capacity to establish clear and enforceable bedtime rules, rules that are nonetheless flexible, can be a significant indicator of the family's adaptability. It is unfortunate when the time for bed becomes a struggle for power instead of a recognition of emerging autonomy.

In the early years, structural clarity is decidedly helpful but rarely sufficient to make bedtime rituals go easily. Parents also need to be comfortable with one another so that the children will be free to retire from their activities when adult time begins. Children who use "just one more story" or "another drink" as a delaying tactic may be

68728

colluding with one or both parents in limiting adult time for intimacy. In ways that are not easily understandable, a child quickly learns that mommy or daddy does not want to be too intimate; so the child's evening interruptions function to stabilize the system by avoiding conflict over adult intimacy needs. Parents who argue about how to handle the request for one more drink of water often do so as a way of coping with their own discomfort with one another.

Ideally, the conversations, stories, and prayers that accompany going to bed are rituals for the termination of the children's day. The bedtime ritual may also provide an occasion for rehearsing the children's next-day activities—such things as when the sitter should come, who will get home first, and who needs to see the dentist. Bedtime rituals are equally important for adults, but establishing a pattern for pillow talk or ways of closing the day will vary greatly and usually requires hard work to maintain. The Pauline admonition not to let the sun go down on our wrath (Eph. 4:26) is sound marital advice: Don't go to bed mad. The prayer that closes the day for Christians in families needs to include confession and thanksgiving as well as intercession.

Functions of Family Rituals

The vitality of family life is in large part determined by the family's capacity to change and adapt. Because people and families change, the roles and rules that govern human interaction in a system must be both clear and flexible. Neither individuals nor families, however, can be infinitely flexible. We have already identified the family's need for human continuity in the midst of change. Stories, traditions, and rituals are means by which families seek to certify their future against the contingencies created by change. Family rituals conserve the past in order to maintain the stability necessary for the family to function as a system. Three particular purposes of family rituals merit special mention.

In the first place, the inheritance that each new generation receives from its past provides an identity and a vocation. Identity is formed by the stories and traditions that pass from one generation to the next. Intergenerational relationships within the family provide each new generation with an emotional inheritance that lends stability and purpose for the future. Families that are separated geographically often become increasingly intentional about collecting or tape-recording family stories as a way of preserving for each new generation a continuity with its past.[5]

This process of passing on a family's legacy for the future is sometimes disrupted by secret keeping. Traditions may be aborted in order to maintain the secret, and the family story is in consequence lost or abbreviated. I once asked an aunt for some information regarding my mother's childhood. "There is no point in digging up old bones," she said. That was that—nothing more was said, but a piece of my own history had been cut out and locked away in the deep, dark past.

A family's identity may be fixed at a particular point or in a particular way in order to make sure that secrets are kept inviolate. The fixed ways of functioning that families develop in order to keep their secrets buried also interrupt the natural transmission of the family's story, by which its identity is formed and its vocation in the world is shaped. Family rituals help to keep that story alive and available for succeeding generations.

The second purpose of family rituals is to mediate between individual and communal needs in order to foster appropriate bonds of intimacy. Every family needs to protect its membership from manipulation and the abuse of autonomy. For that purpose we have insisted on clear boundaries. Rituals are necessary in order to ensure privacy. Likewise a family system must structure rituals for the purpose of being together so that moments of intimacy may happen. Rituals do not guarantee closeness in a family. Some family rituals connected with play or lovemaking may actually make intimacy difficult if they are rigidly enforced. When they function well, however, family rituals make intimacy possible by ensuring accessibility. It is unwise to kiss your spouse only when you feel like it, or make love only when you are already close, or hug your children only when they seem particularly lovable. Rituals like going to Grandma's are important precisely because they do not depend on good intentions or warm feelings. Human systems need rituals that structure accessibility in order that gracious moments of intimacy may happen.

The third purpose of rituals is to mark out individual development in such a way that a family can adapt to individual changes.

Families may have ceremonies surrounding the start of school, the beginning of menstruation, the receiving of a promotion, the recognition of achievement, or leaving home. Every major event of an individual's life is in a sense a family affair. Rituals are one way by which the family as a system can adjust to the changes that will be occurring in its life because of the ritual event. Families that function best will never allow the system's needs for stability to disrupt the individuating moment for one of its members. Rituals that work best will honor autonomy and celebrate community simultaneously.

Rituals and Pastoral Care

In chapter 2 I identified five epochs in the family life cycle that mark out periods of significant change in a family's history. In each of these five epochs, as suggested in the table below, there are rituals in the church's life that correspond to the family's principal task. Pastoral work is enhanced by these ritual moments. They provide a structured access to people at those times of transition when family systems are likely to get stuck. They offer an opportunity for the pastoral care of families that encourages and supports adaptability. If the family is able to adapt to the transitions precipitated by individual change, that very adaptation will in turn create an atmosphere conducive to the kind of individual growth that can proceed without fear of jeopardizing the stability of the family unit.

I agree with Murray Bowen's suggestion that a life-cycle format may provide "one of the most practical and effective ways to help people find a quicker understanding of the family as a unit."[6] Understanding the family life cycle also provides the pastor with a framework for thinking about how ordinary pastoral interventions around the church's ritual life correspond to critical moments of transition in the family's life history. The pastoral care of families begins with attention to the family's developmental tasks, which in each epoch correspond to the church's rituals. The ritual life of the church is generally understood to focus on incorporation into being-in-community: (1) we are baptized into the whole company of the faithful in the context of a particular believing community; (2) the Eucharist is a community meal; (3) it is the community as a whole that confirms an adult believer or welcomes a confessing Christian. Although our communities change and enlarge, they are never

Epoch	Task	Pastoral Opportunities
Forming the family	Setting boundaries between the generations and within the marriage that are clear but permeable	The focus of pre-marital pastoral work is that leaving comes before cleaving
Enlarging the family	A craziness about kids that makes it possible to tran-scend the inconvenience of child rearing	Pastoral visitation at the time of baptism should include a focus on the family's adaptation to the child
Expanding the family	The family needs to be a system that is open enough for people to discuss their own gifts and distinct self	Participation in first communion and confirmation are ways by which the church's rituals enhance the process of individuation
Extending the family	Parents and children alike need to understand that children need to leave home in order to come home again	Visiting with parents after the wedding is a way to help them let go of the child who has gone
Re-forming the family	New intimacy in the original marital pair creates free-dom for all members of the system	Pastoral intervention is necessary because the death of a parent may have a profound impact on middle-aged sons and daughters

eliminated; the Christian is forever understood as part of a people. This emphasis on the sociality of life, however, is not uniquely Christian; human life at its best and deepest is always and irrevocably corporate.

The rituals of the church are also moments that foster individuation: (1) we are particularized by being named in our baptism; (2) the Christian affirmation of faith is always an "I believe"; (3) throughout the Christian life, each of us is identified as a distinct and unique child of God. The family dialectic of being separate together also occurs in the ritual life of the church. The Christian life, even in its rituals, is always both individual and corporate. Understood in this way, the rituals of the church can undergird the family's task of helping people learn how to be together separately. At the same time, the rituals of the family that maintain this same dialectic between separateness and togetherness also make it possible for people to claim their uniqueness as a gift from God for service in the world.

CHAPTER 8

Perspectives for the Pastoral Care of Families

THE HELPER'S FAMILY OF ORIGIN

In the Introduction I suggested that an individual's experience in his or her family of origin is the primary authority for understanding the dynamics of family life. Pastors and counselors particularly need to bear this in mind. Whatever else we learn or determine about the family is measured against the lingering influences of our original family. For example, the fact that the theology for the family presented here is tilted slightly in favor of individuation is not unrelated to my own personal struggles for differentiation from my family of origin.

There is, similarly, a connection between our particular ways of helping and the roles we played in our families of origin. It should be clear that in spite of its diminishing influence in the larger society the family is still, for those who belong to it, a powerful emotional system. Unless we self-consciously and intentionally choose to change, we are likely to minister to families in ways that are similar to the ways in which we functioned in our own families of origin.

The kind of role we played in our families affects our pastoral impulses. It is probably even instrumental in our being called to be helpers. As the oldest in my family, the one identified as being responsible, I join a countless host of individuals with similar family backgrounds who have chosen a career or profession that will continue to make it possible for us to be responsible for the lives of other people.

Some people become pastors or helping persons because their parents, out of gratitude for a miraculous birth or an extraordinary healing, gave them back to God. It may be easy for such individuals to hope for miraculous changes in a troubled family, but it is not easy for such persons not to help. They are compelled to care out of a sense of gratitude.

Others may have chosen a helping role as a kind of penance—in order to pay off a debt they feel for having failed in their first assignment to be a healer. Such failure might have been felt when a parent's marriage, which one had been expected to save, was finally dissolved. Or when one's mother, whom one had been expected to rescue from depression, finally had to be institutionalized. Or when a sibling, whom one was assigned to teach and make smart, finally failed a grade in school. Such family experiences can produce, especially in those who later become pastors and helpers, an over-whelming need to save—lest the debt be increased.

Sometimes their families of origin can impart a special blessing to a pastor or helper. This is most clearly seen in family histories that show how the mantle has been passed from great-grandpa Gardner or from aunt Lillian to the one who has decided to be pastor. People who have received such mantles from their families of origin are likely to exercise the authority of a "chosen one."

Knowing how we functioned in our own families of origin can help us understand how we are likely to engage with troubled families. Families are often delighted to find a healer who might take away the pain without changing the system, or someone who will take over responsibility for the family's well-being and at whom the family can later vent its anger when "things don't get better." If, in our family of origin, we were the peacemaker in marital conflicts, we will need to be careful about taking sides in a troubled marriage. We are easily "hooked" by familiar roles and patterns that limit our ability to be an effective agent of change.

This focus on our family of origin involves more than an ordinary concern for pastoral self-understanding. Indeed it marks a shift away from the presumed neutrality of the helper. As pastors, it is impossible, and even undesirable, for us *not* to join the families with whom we work. Even if we choose not to, we inevitably become a part of the family's web. We will be quoted in family disputes, and even when we are not present our authority will be invoked for the sake of discipline. The critical question is not whether but how we join the family, how we enter the complicated web of interactions in a manner that can evoke change. In order to effect change we must join the family on our own terms, not theirs. Therefore we need to be aware of our own family roles and interactional patterns lest we follow unwittingly the impulses that were fostered within us by our original families.

THINKING INTERACTIONALLY

Learning how to work with families is initially more a matter of perspective than a method of intervention. It involves a movement toward thinking about people not just as individuals with a particular identity, but also as units within a system that also has an identifiable life of its own. The family is the primary human system. Thinking about people systemically or interactionally means seeing individuals—even those who live alone—in relation to their family as the primary emotional system. Our family of origin affords us our first experience of living in a system in which all the parts interrelate. Throughout our lives, even if we remain single, we live in families, and our families live in us.

The shift toward a systemic or interactional way of thinking about people does not occur easily. Individualism is deeply ingrained in Western thought; it permeates our art, politics, and religion. Respect for the value of each individual is undoubtedly one of the major contributions of Western civilization; here neither the corporation, the government, the faceless bureaucracy, nor the crowd is of greater worth than the individual. Most radically expressed, to be an individual is to stand out from the community. Because the therapeutic tradition from Freud to Rogers has been shaped by the individualistic bias of Western culture, it is not easy to shift to a more interactional way of thinking.

Although systems thinking may seem strange to our individualistically oriented Western ears, it really involves the reintroduction of a perspective on being-in-community that is as old as ancient Israel. Indeed, the anthropology of family-systems theory is more compatible with the Hebrew tradition than with the Greek-dominated anthropology of Western Christianity. Human beings are linked together in communities not just because of those early attachments that make bonding essential for survival, but because we are communal creatures by nature. Learning to think interactionally involves for the West a new epistemology in which some of the old rules no longer apply.[1]

Taking our bearings more from a communal than an individual anthropology is likely to change our assumptions about the purpose of the family. If one regards human beings as naturally community-minded, then it is easier to think about the family as both the context for individuation and the source of social stability. If people are community-minded only after the family has socialized their natural self-centeredness through disciplined training, then it would follow that the family's primary task of socialization is to curtail solipsism and keep self-oriented impulses in check. However, selfishness is not the only expression of sin. Too much togetherness, if it prohibits individuation, is equally sinful. The anthropology that undergirds a systems approach to the care of families holds that being together is as natural as being separate. Paradoxically, it is only as our anthropology is sufficiently communal or systemic that the family is likely to become a place in which individual uniqueness is nurtured.

A systems approach to the family is a way of thinking about persons that seeks to foster the interdependence between individuals and their significant communities. All of us live within a social context. Our interaction with the world around us is shaped by the lingering impact of our families of origin. Intrapsychic conflicts not only have systemic origins; they often involve an ongoing struggle with the family within us, long after we have physically left home. Because thinking in terms of systems involves a change in perspective, *what* we see is more important than *whom* we counsel. What distinguishes the systems perspective is a recognition of the interactional character of human life, which is an extension of the interdependence of all creation.

> Pauline is a twenty-seven-year-old single woman who had not lived at home for nearly ten years. She first left home in order to attend college, not long after her mother's death. Despite obvious intellectual gifts, Pauline had settled on a job that exchanged stability for stimulation. She now lived alone in a modest one-room apartment in a large city and, although she had a number of friends and was active in her church, she described her life as lonely and pointless.
>
> After a recurrence of depression, Pauline took a leave of absence from work, returned home, and began outpatient treatment. She was given medication that altered her emotional state, and vocational guid-

ance to help her deal with her job dissatisfaction. These measures seemed to provide some relief but they did not address her lingering malaise. Pauline then began exploring issues related to her family of origin and the death of her mother.

Although her siblings were geographically dispersed, Pauline was able to gather them for a meeting with her pastor. At that counseling session, two things became evident: It was Pauline more than anyone else who kept alive the grief for her mother's death; in that sense there was good cause for her depression. It was also evident that the family had been unwilling to relieve Pauline of her burden of carrying the family pain. It was while telephoning her siblings in order to arrange the family gathering that Pauline discovered that others in the family too were suffering from a pain they were unwilling to share. Following that discovery, though the system apparently would not change, Pauline's relation to it now could.

Subsequent to that significant family meeting, Pauline was urged by the pastor to visit her mother's grave and write about the visit to her siblings, who over the period of eleven years had never once been to visit the site where their mother was buried. The intent of that assignment was to help Pauline with her own lingering grief and then to share some of that grief with the rest of the family. Although Pauline did not receive acknowledgement from her brothers or sisters that they had received her expression of belated grief and were willing to share it, Pauline began to alter her own perception of her place in the family and to act accordingly.

When the systems perspective is used in counseling with individuals, the primary goal is to change their ways of interacting with their family. If the family too changes, that is a bonus. Pauline became aware that her depression was a family affair, and although she was unable to convince her family of the benefits of thinking interactionally, she herself continued—with the encouragement of her pastor—to respond to her family in ways that gradually diminished her sense of powerlessness at being the only bearer of the family's buried grief.

CIRCULAR CAUSALITY

Thinking about people interactionally changes our approach from focusing on the individual psyche to focusing on the system. It also replaces linear causality with circular causality. Our persistence in asking "why" questions, even in circumstances when that seems inappropriate, is not simply a matter of curiosity; it is a clue to the intensity with which we are likely to hold on to assumptions about linear causality. Because interdependence is a mark of the family as a human system, it is impossible to think about causality in a linear way. Thinking interactionally means that when a family is troubled, everybody is responsible. Because of the mutuality of influence, it is probably more accurate to say that the system is responsible for the system's trouble.

This shift toward circular causality has three consequences for pastoral work with families. First of all, with respect to divorce it eliminates the idea that there is an innocent party. Although churches no longer support the idea that blame can be located in just one person and that only the so-called innocent party may remarry, it is still common for people being divorced to want to believe that they are the ones who had been innocently victimized by their partner. The insistence on innocence in family or marital trouble prevents the realization of forgiveness. People who are "innocent" need no forgiveness because they are "victims." People who have been labeled as victimizers frequently insist that they will ask forgiveness only if the so-called victim will acknowledge his or her fault.

The process of healing after divorce can begin only after both parties acknowledge responsibility for the demise of the marriage. An insistence of innocence precludes forgiveness; instead, the victim hopes for sympathy and looks for confirmatory allies. Pastors who want to be sympathetic may find themselves all too rapidly drawn into the orbit of the self-appointed victim. For that reason, it is as important as it is difficult for helpers always to explore the other side of every question and accusation in a family dispute. "Why did my husband have an affair?" becomes also "How long have you wanted your husband to leave?" Such a question can of course evoke more resistance than is useful. Alternatively therefore the pastor may simply observe: "It is difficult sometimes to be certain whether one wants a husband to stay or to go." Where the insistence of innocence lingers, it can become a way of life whereby individuals and families avoid accountability or responsibility by accusing others and the world around them.

> It was perfectly clear to Sylvia that she wanted to divorce Richard. Richard, however, still in love with her and determined to continue the relationship, was unwilling to take any action toward terminating the marriage. For a variety of reasons Sylvia did not want to assume responsibility for the divorce. In order to move him to action Sylvia became

careless about her affairs and cruel in her relationship to Richard. His assumed righteousness was magnified by the benevolence with which he responded to her philandering. Thus the process of divorcing was prolonged in a way that was detrimental to everyone in the family—all in order that Sylvia could avoid guilt and Richard could presume innocence.

The introduction of circular causality not only puts an end to the myth of innocence in troubled families. It also, in the second place, allows the pastor more freedom to suggest to the family creative alternatives. One can "play around with possibilities" if the seriousness of linear thinking has been modified by the perspective of circular causality. As long as "this" does not simply and directly cause "that," families in conflict can have more freedom to explore possible resolutions that do not create winners and losers. If the crisis can be understood as the result of a failure, then the entire family can be invited to redirect its creative energies away from blaming and toward a solution of the crisis.

Third, the shift toward circular causality enhances our understanding of corporate sin as over against individual sin. Families sin as surely as the people within them. By insisting that it is the *family* that is troubled, we shift the locus of blame from individuals to the organism as a whole. This focus on the organism as a whole does not eliminate individual accountability; it simply means that in a functioning human system, such as the family, it is not enough to blame one person for all the trouble. Nor is it necessarily useful to fault each individual. The family as such sins.

The interdependence of all things and the mutual influence or effect that each individual has on every other and on the whole undermine some of our traditional theological assumptions about fault and guilt. An individualistic understanding of guilt is not terribly useful, either for effecting change in a family or for understanding how a family functions. People are nonetheless likely to hold on to old assumptions about linear causality because they find it uncomfortable always to be accountable themselves for a family's sin. And because it is impossible to fix blame outside ourselves, we are of necessity thrown back on the dynamic of forgiveness as the Christian tradition's central contribution to living in a family.

CHANGE AS GOAL

Regarding change as a goal for the pastoral care of families is consistent with an understanding of creation in which change is normative. Families become troubled because they cannot cope with the change that is a necessary part of any organism's life. Denial of the inevitability of change often precipitates family crisis. A family may enforce rigid and unrealistic rules in order to keep children from growing up and going away. It may elect a scapegoat in order to divert attention away from necessary change. It may have developed fixed patterns of communication in order to avoid the grief that always accompanies change. Families become troubled because of the patterns they create in an effort to avoid inevitable or necessary change.

When a family is in crisis, the needed pastoral intervention must be primarily in the interest of change. Even families that seek help, however, will be ambivalent about change. They will resist any change that would substantially alter the family equilibrium. They would prefer to have a change in the identified problem or scapegoat—so that the system as a whole would not need to change. However, by the time a family asks for help, someone or something has usually made change no longer optional; it is essential for its own survival that the family alter its patterns of interaction.

Families often find themselves stuck with a pattern of interacting so that the more they change the more they stay the same. In such instances the members of the family keep changing roles, but nothing new happens. What is needed in this case is a change in change itself—actually a change in the fundamental rules that govern the system—so that, for example, a child might get credit for actually practicing the piano even if she doesn't *want* to. What happens is more important than why it happens.[2]

Karl had been married only eight months when it dawned on him that he was beginning to withdraw from Pamela. The emotional demands of being married were more than he had bargained for. For Karl home had always been a quiet, well-ordered oasis in an otherwise chaotic world. By contrast, Pamela's family had majored in disorder. At first, Karl had been intrigued by a wife who seemed always to live on the edge of disaster. Before long, however, he yearned to replace his whirlwind home with the clean, well-lighted place that his mother had always provided. At that point he sought help from the pastor who had married them.

Seeking help was in itself a large step for Karl. Self-sufficiency had long been a dominant motif in the orderliness of his whole family; his Norwegian grandmother had had a favorite maxim: "Every tub must stand on its own bottom." Thus Karl was actually breaking a family rule just by asking for help. When Karl at length admitted openly his discomfort with his family's traditional commitment to orderliness, his mother felt freed to admit that she herself had never wanted that to be her primary preoccupation; it was the fastidiousness of her Norwegian mother that had set the tone for the entire family. By seeking help, and by telling his family he had, Karl effected a change that had widespread consequences. He changed a rule that had governed the whole system.

Interdependence, we have noted, is characteristic of family life. Because of that, change in one individual will have consequences for the entire system. Small change, it is said, makes for large change. That is a hopeful word for families in trouble, who often assume that they will need to make what they regard as an impossible major overhaul. One small change, though, may be enough to alter counterproductive interactional patterns. Sometimes it suffices, as in Karl's case, just to make a public acknowledgement that the family is troubled and needs help. Even though the change in question may appear to be small, pastors need to recognize that anything new in the family is likely to be perceived as frightening. Because of their fear of change and of the unknown, families resist change even when they are admittedly miserable. From a pastoral perspective, then, every change, however small, must be tended carefully.

SOURCES OF CHANGE

Pastoral Presence

The presence of the pastor in relation to a family is a primary source of change. Family interactions will change simply because another person has been added to the system. For this reason a helping person is never neutral in relation to the family. The way in which the pastor enters the system becomes itself a critical determinant in the effectiveness of the help offered with a view to facilitating change. Pastoral work with families is complicated by the other relationships the pastor may have previously established with people in the parish. The pastor may already have been looked upon as a surrogate parent, as a replacement for a beloved child, or as a substitute spouse. Pastors must take into account their own prior relationships with the family as well as the family roles originally encountered upon entering the family system at a time of crisis. When a family seeks help, the pastor must usually join the system in a new way.

The first contact with a family seeking help can either reinforce old patterns of relating among the members or provide the occasion for change. The presence of the pastor will be a catalyst for change only if it does not simply reinforce existent patterns within the system. From the moment of the initial telephone call requesting help, or of the first casual comment following a church meeting, the pastor must be in charge. Only the helping person who is able to take charge of the process of joining the family will find it possible to modify the use of power in that system. The helping person needs to win the initial struggle for power if power is eventually to be redistributed more evenly within the family. Who is present for the first family meeting, who tells the family problem, who sits next to whom, who sets the agenda—are all issues around which helpers have opportunity to establish their authority.

Effective work with a family requires a willingness on the part of a pastor to exercise appropriate authority. For a pastor this process of joining the family as the one in charge can be complicated by existent limits on the exercise of pastoral authority. Where the pastor does not take charge of the helping process, however, change is not likely to occur. A systems perspective on family care is useful because it reintroduces questions about the relationship between authority and the exercise of pastoral care.

Redefining the Problem

Although helping persons join the family as a functioning member, they must remain sufficiently outside the system to be able to reinterpret the problem that the family itself presents. Such redefinition provides a second source of change within the helping process.

The family is likely to describe its trouble in a way that limits the possibilities for change in favor of the status quo. One individual will often be identified as the family's problem. If Melissa would stop skipping school, or if David would stop nagging, or if Monica would stop running around, or if Father were less depressed, or if Calvin would do his homework, or if Mother stayed home more—then the family would be better.

We have already identified (in chapter 5) this phenomenon of scapegoating as the system's mechanism for maintaining equilibrium. Because the family often persists in its understanding of the family's problem, the task of reframing or redefining the problem in relation to the system as a whole is a delicate one. The reframing needs to be done without either disparaging the problem or discrediting the family member assigned to present it.

Reframing or redefining the problem has several purposes. A reinterpretation of the situation can create new freedom simply by helping people think in terms of the family as a whole rather than just the individuals within it. Redefining the problem can reduce the power of the one first presenting it to determine how the family as a whole will function and how the counseling will proceed. Such redefinition takes pressure off the family scapegoat. It expands the possibilities for a resolution of the family's difficulty. It may even mobilize the family to act as a unit in opposing the helper who, as an outsider, simply "cannot understand what we have been through."

> Chester was the fourth in a family of four children. Except for the second daughter all the children had speech difficulties like those of their father. The family was sent for counseling because Chester had become troublesome in school, was constantly fighting with his older brother, disobeyed his parents, and generally made trouble wherever he went. Chester was seven years old. His father and mother fought constantly about disciplining the children and about managing the family business. The system was so enmeshed that every fight was a family affair. The pastor reframed the problem by suggesting that the family was so busy fighting that they did not have time to be sad. Being sad was a private matter. In order to break the family's pattern of interacting, the pastor suggested that they designate a "sadness jar" into which family members could put notes about things that made them lonely or sad. These could then be shared at the next family session.

The art of reframing requires creativity and gentleness. A family has generally made an emotional investment in its definition of the problem, and they are reluctant to give it up. Family members must set aside self-perceptions as well as perceptions generated by the family as a whole in order to accept the reframing. Chester's family was intrigued by the prospect that they might begin to do something together besides fight. Gentleness and subtle creativity on the part of the pastor can help to make reframing acceptable as a new way of understanding the family's problem.

The person who has entered the system in order to help is able to see and redefine the family's problem in a new way only by also remaining outside the system. Creativity requires distance. Those who are drawn into the family's web can usually imagine only such ways out of the trouble as are likely to perpetuate the family's dysfunctional patterns. The helping person's imaginative capacity depends on being able to see the family as a whole and from the outside. Sometimes it is advantageous to begin with seemingly ridiculous redefinitions of the problem, so that in the end the preferred reframing will seem reasonable after all. And always creativity in the art of reframing needs to be combined with gentleness.

Altering Alliances

In addition to the helper's presence and redefinition of the presenting problem, change may be evoked within the family by rearranging alliances. According to the principle of interdependence, a family functions best when it has within it no fixed alliances. Boundaries between members of a family and between the family and its environment are permeable precisely in order to enhance availability for everyone. Fixed alliances exclude. Altering a dysfunctional alliance or unsettling a fixed interactional pattern is thus a third source of change for the family.

PASTORAL AUTHORITY

Intervention in a family in order to bring about change in its interactional patterns can occur in a variety of ways. It may happen in the counseling session itself. More frequently, it will take the form of homework assignments given to the family for individual and joint work between sessions. In making such assignments it is essential that the helping person demonstrate both clarity and confidence. For the pastor who works with families this means the appropriate use of authority in the interests of change.

> Marian and Daniel had been separated for nearly four months before the pastor's home visit to Marian. At the first meeting, the pastor suggested that she *might* eventually want Daniel to move back home for the sake of enhanced opportunity to work on the relationship. By the time of the next interview, Daniel had already returned home, much to the delight of their ten-year-old daughter Nancy. At the third meeting it became clear to the pastor that both Marian and Daniel had close emotional ties to their families of origin, but very little intimacy in their own marital relationship. Even though the pastor wisely structured the setting and regulated the conversation so that Daniel and Marian would have to engage one another, they consistently found ways to deflect their intimacy through the pastor.
>
> When their daughter joined the family meeting, the pastor became aware that the emotional bond between Nancy and her father excluded Marian. Throughout the session, Nancy directed her attentions to her father; he reciprocated to the exclusion of his wife. At the close of the interview, the pastor assigned Daniel and Marian the task of eating out alone. In subsequent meetings, as it became clearer to the couple that Daniel's inappropriate intimacy with Nancy was disruptive to the marriage, the pastor assigned other tasks designed to bolster the marital alliance by setting clearer boundaries between the generations.

It is important that when tasks are assigned they be small and achievable. The pastor's directions to Daniel and Marian simply asked them to do what couples or parents might ordinarily do anyway. It is equally necessary that the assignments be made clearly, authoritatively, and without extensive explanation. When people want to know why they are being asked to do something, the helper or pastor can simply reply: "It seems like a good idea," or: "It can't do any harm." The focus for the moment should be on the helper's authority rather than on justifying arguments. It is the exercise of pastoral authority that introduces the possibility of change within a family system. People are most likely to trust a pastor who has strength.

It has been suggested that pastors are limited in their work with families because they do not have enough distance to be objectively authoritative, and even if a pastor were able to be authoritative in relation to family care that people might have difficulty accepting the objective exercise of authority which may be needed to evoke change. The caution is both real and overstated. One of the real difficulties of pastoral care of any kind is that ordinary prior pastoral relationships may preclude the kind of distance that is necessary for effective family counseling. Yet people whose families are in trouble are often more willing to grant authority than pastors are to receive and exercise it. The pastoral reticence is an appropriate hedge against abuse, but it can also limit a pastor's effectiveness in helping families to change. It is most important to remember that our very presence with a family, despite the limits to our pastoral authority, can itself evoke change so long as we can remain outside the family's web.

PASTORAL INITIATIVE

Parish visitation is an honored privilege available to pastors as to no other caretaking professionals. Pastoral initiative in this regard, however, has for a variety of reasons diminished in our time as a matter of common pastoral practice. If my own parish experience is any indicator, that decline is neither surprising nor simply the consequence of sloth. I was not prepared for all the pain, sorrow, and conflict I encountered when I opened the doors of homes in my parish. I found it easier just to stop calling altogether than to deal with such suffering day after day. Moreover, the parish call at the pastor's initiative has traditionally been a stylized encounter, generally structured to exclude deep probing or a therapeutically oriented interaction.

The recent development of the home visit as a significant method in family therapy provides new impetus for our reconsidering the ancient privilege of pastoral initiative. Therapists are discovering what pastors have always known—that meeting people in their homes enhances care. The emotional impact of seeing something at firsthand can often reveal the nature of the family situation in a way not otherwise available. The physical household, its contents, and the rules for their use amount to a vast and living representation of the psychosocial life of the family. Because welcoming the pastor into the home is also like showing hospitality to strangers, it can be an observable indicator of the system's openness and adaptability. A home visit can reveal how the family's habitat is created, how the system maintains a balance between public and private space, and how the outside world is kept out or brought into the home environment.

Effective pastoral care of families, however, involves more than simply gathering information. The privilege of visitation requires the careful and gentle use of authority. Pastors whose calling on families has been sensitized by a systems perspective may do little more than augment the frustration unless, within the family visit, they are able to take some initiative for introducing a concern prompted by intuition and confirmed by observation. Taking initiative includes a willingness to be active in pastoral relationships. It can mean, for example, asking about the well-being of a family whose daughter seems troubled at youth meetings, or inquiring about a father who has suddenly stopped singing in the choir, or seeking to reconnect with someone who has become estranged from the parish system. Care for people always includes respect for their reluctance to consider painful subjects and for their rejection of our intuitions. But care also means being willing to take the initiative, even in the midst of the family.

The pastor who visits a family in its home is first of all a guest. The family will show hospitality in its own way in order to make the pastoral guest feel at home. Although it is necessary for the pastor to be a receptive guest, that alone is not enough. Pastoral calling of any kind becomes more than a matter of public relations or social connecting at the point where the pastor becomes the host. The presence of Christ in human life as both guest and host is the paradigm for our pastoral visitation.

By taking the initiative to become the host in a family's own home the pastor makes it possible for each family member to tell his or her own story. The good host is a person who does not ignore anyone's contribution. Being a good host means forming an alliance with the disenfranchised and neglected individuals in the family. Each individual's unique gift is intentionally and explicitly added to the whole life of the family organism. Pastoral initiative with families does not mean a license to do counseling unawares. It is rather the recovery of a vital sense of being a participant with people in their struggle to discover their own gifts and to find courage to become autonomous disciples in the world for Christ's sake.

Despite our desire to help troubled families, and despite the obvious need in families today for healing and wholeness, pastors must remain free of the family's emotional web if they are to be free to offer what limited help they can. Troubled families will want to be told how to live, and our desire to help may prompt us willingly to tell them how to be or what to do. If we are to avoid this trap of taking responsibility for the family's well-being, we will have to remember constantly our own powerlessness.

Our first purpose in being with a family is to connect with them, not to save them. With each family it is essential to make a connection at the beginning of the pastoral visit. People in families need to believe that their pain has been heard and understood, even if it is eventually reframed. The process of making connections with each family member is enhanced by the helper's ability to empathize. Empathy communicates understanding and builds trust, but it does not necessarily evoke change. It is helpful, but it is not enough. Moreover, because of the emotional power of the family system, unbounded empathy may result in insufficient distance from the family. We can help families change only if we stay outside the system even while we participate in it.

A THEOLOGICAL DIALECTIC FOR THE PASTORAL CARE OF FAMILIES

Caring for families is a complicated enterprise in our time. Recent changes in family patterning have produced an unsettling diversity of family structures. Not all of the changes have been constructive for life together in the family. The increase in divorce is an alarming indication of how difficult it is to keep a balance between autonomy and mutuality. There are signs of parental negligence that point to a disregard of the family's obligation to ensure the future of humankind. The increase in family violence gives evidence of internal stress in the nuclear system. Issues such as the advisability and adequacy of day care and the prevention of teenage pregnancy prompt fierce public debate over the role of the family as a guarantor of the common good. In addition, the growing isolation of the family is likely to create more problems than it solves. Ours is indeed a troubled time for the family.

Despite the seeming chaos created by the modern pluralism of values and diversity of structures, we cannot do without the family as such—or something like it. The family has survived revolutionary changes throughout its history. Moreover the diversity of family structure is a sign of God's extravagant care. The family as a human system is inextricably linked to a creation that is yet unfinished. Change and diversity, however troubling, are characteristics of the family as a part of that creation. Our pastoral interventions will be made in the interest of evoking those structural and interactional changes that can help the family become a workshop for change.

Pastors are able to respond to families freely because they realize that the family is not an end in itself. How a pastor responds to crisis in a particular family is influenced by the recognition that while creation requires the family to be a context for criticism and care, Christian discipleship transcends this necessity from creation. There is truth in the absurdity of the gospel's demand that faithfulness to Jesus set parents and children at sword's point. To regard every follower of Jesus as my brother or sister is an impossible ideal. Yet to be a disciple of Christ is to recognize ever-enlarging communities of concern. Christians are obligated not to take the family too seriously lest it impede our service in the world for Christ's sake.

Our intent throughout these chapters has been to develop a theology for the family, one that will inform and be informed by our pastoral work with families. Pastors have unique access to people during the expected and unexpected crises that occur within their family life cycle. Most pastors have neither the time nor the training to do therapy with families. The systems approach to family therapy does, however, introduce a perspective as well as interventive techniques that are readily applicable in pastoral care. Learning how to think about people interactionally moreover provides a perspective that has potential not just for pastoral care but for the whole of pastoral ministry.[3]

Pastoral initiative in relation to family life is taken ultimately for the sake of individuals. Our pastoral work is informed by the conviction that families need to be open and interdependent systems, capable of fostering the growth toward autonomy that occurs only in those communities which can love and let go. Belonging and autonomy are both vital for human identity. Learning how to live together separately constitutes a lifelong agenda, the first lessons of which are experienced in the family. The systems perspective on family life enables us to acknowledge that growth toward autonomy is most likely to occur in families where the rules are flexible, the roles interchangeable, and the rituals dependable. It is the call to discipleship, however, that pushes us out of such nurturing communities into those ever-enlarging circles of interaction and concern in which God continues to make all things new.

Notes

INTRODUCTION

1. Learning how to live together separately is admittedly a middle-class luxury. There are many societies today in which basic survival is still the organizing principle for what a family is and does. Although my understanding of the family has been shaped primarily by a white, middle-class experience, I have found that the basic themes here proposed do have cross-cultural applicability.

2. For a fuller discussion of Luther's views on the family see William H. Lazareth, *Luther on the Christian Home* (Philadelphia: Fortress Press, 1960).

3. Clarissa W. Atkinson, "American Families and 'the American Family': Myths and Realities," *Harvard Divinity Bulletin* 12/2 (December 1981–January 1982): 13.

CHAPTER 1

1. *Choices in Childlessness,* The Report of a Working Party under the auspices of the Free Church Federal Council and the British Council of Churches, March 1982, p. 24.

2. Ibid., 31. See also Karen Lebacqz, ed., *Genetics, Ethics, and Parenthood* (New York: Pilgrim Press, 1983).

CHAPTER 2

1. Tamara K. Hareven, "Family Time and Historical Time," *Daedalus* 106/2 (Spring 1977): 69.

2. Philip J. Hefner, "Towards a New Doctrine of Man: The Relationship of Man and Nature," in *The Future of Empirical Theology* (Chicago: University of Chicago Press, 1969).

3. Theodore Lidz, *The Family and Human Adaptation* (New York: International Universities Press, 1963), 29.

4. Pierre Teilhard de Chardin, *Man's Place in Nature,* trans. Rene Hague (New York: Harper & Row, 1966), 107–8.

5. Don Browning, *Pluralism and Personality* (Lewisburg, Pa.: Bucknell University Press, 1980), esp. 19–42.

6. Norman Paul, "The Use of Empathy in the Resolution of Grief," *Perspectives in Biology and Medicine* (Autumn, 1967): 161. For a fuller clinical

development of this theme, see Norman L. Paul and Betty Byfield Paul, *A Marital Puzzle* (New York: W. W. Norton, 1975).

7. Lawrence Stone, *The Family, Sex and Marriage in England, 1500–1800* (New York: Penguin Books, 1979), esp. 149–80.

8. Edward Shorter, *The Making of the Modern Family* (New York: Basic Books, 1975).

9. Jack O. Bradt, "The Family with Young Children," in *The Family Life Cycle*, ed. Elizabeth A. Carter and Monica McGoldrick (New York: Gardner Press, 1980), 126.

CHAPTER 3

1. Christopher Lasch, *Haven in a Heartless World* (New York: Basic Books, 1977), 18 and 19. Lasch develops the idea that the primary responsibility for socializing children has shifted from the family to society. "The socialization of reproduction completed the process begun by the socialization of production itself—that is, by industrialization" (18).

2. I have identified this "crisis of competence" in an essay "The Family Under Stress: A Crisis of Purpose," in *Moral Issues and Christian Response*, 3d ed., ed. Paul T. Jersild and Dale A. Johnson (New York: Holt, Rinehart, & Winston, 1983), 114–24.

3. This position, held by a number of social analysts, has most recently been developed in Brigitte Berger and Peter L. Berger, *The War Over the Family* (New York: Doubleday Anchor Books, 1983). The Bergers strongly embrace and advocate the traditional family as the repository of important personal and social virtues.

4. Jürgen Moltmann, *The Future of Creation* (Philadelphia: Fortress Press, 1979), 118.

CHAPTER 4

1. Pierre Teilhard de Chardin, *The Phenomenon of Man*, trans. Bernard Wall (New York: Harper & Brothers, 1959), 48.

2. Gustaf Wingren, *Credo*, trans. Edgar M. Carlson (Minneapolis: Augsburg Publishing House, 1981), 53ff.

3. Claus Westermann, *Creation*, trans. John J. Scullion, S.J. (Philadelphia: Fortress Press, 1974), 86.

4. Salvador Minuchin, *Families and Family Therapy* (Cambridge: Harvard University Press, 1974).

5. Valerie Saiving, "The Human Situation: A Feminine View," in *Womenspirit Rising*, ed. Carol P. Christ and Judith Plaskow (New York and San Francisco: Harper & Row, 1979), 25–42.

6. Frederick Buechner, *Godric* (New York: Atheneum, 1981), 48.

7. Augustus Y. Napier and Carl A. Whitaker have described this dialectic clearly in *The Family Crucible* (New York: Harper & Row, 1978). "We feel that the family's capacity to be intimate and caring and their capacity to be separate and divergent increase in careful synchrony. People can't risk

being close unless they have the ability to be separate—it's too frightening to be deeply involved if you aren't sure you can be separate and stand on your own. They also can't risk being truly divergent and separate if they are unable to count on a residual warmth and caring to keep them together. The more forceful and independent they become, the easier it is to risk being intimate and close. The more closeness, the easier it is to risk independence" (93).

8. Walter Brueggemann, "The Covenanted Family—A Zone for Humanness," *Journal of Current Social Issues* 14/1 (Winter 1977): 18.

CHAPTER 5

1. Paul Tillich, *Systematic Theology*, vol. 1 (Chicago: University of Chicago Press, 1951), 176–77.

2. The extent to which the process of leaving home is a serious issue for modern families is reflected in two significant books on the theme. Jay Haley, *Leaving Home* (New York: McGraw-Hill, 1980); and Helm Stierlin, *Separating Parents and Adolescents* (New York: Quadrangle, 1974).

3. The theme of accommodation as a necessary factor for family life is persuasively developed by Nathan Ackerman, *Treating the Troubled Family* (New York: Basic Books, 1966).

CHAPTER 6

1. Wingren in *Credo* states: "The primitive Christian way of looking upon individual differences as an *enhancement* of the oneness instead of a diminution of it, involves an interpretation of originality and individuality, and gives an importance to divergences which has hardly ever been realized in the Christian church to this day" (153).

2. Rene Dubos, *Celebrations of Life* (New York: McGraw-Hill, 1981), 115.

3. Alice S. Rossi, "A Biosocial Perspective on Parenting," *Daedulus*, 106/2 (Spring 1977): 3.

4. Ibid., 25.

CHAPTER 7

1. Rossi, "Biosocial Perspective," 18. Since Edmund O. Wilson's ground-breaking 1975 text, *Sociobiology: The New Synthesis*, a body of literature has emerged in support of the thesis that altruism in the natural world is at heart a selfish genetic ploy. Social organization depends on the satisfaction of individual need and on an environment in which needs are satisfied and dangers avoided.

2. Although the focus of rules may shift from structure to communication patterns, family therapists agree on the necessity of rules for regulating a family system. See especially Virginia Satir, *Peoplemaking* (Palo Alto, Calif: Science and Behavior Books, 1972), 96–111.

3. David Cooper, *The Death of the Family* (Harmondsworth, Eng.: Penguin Press, 1971).

4. Edwin H. Friedman, "Systems and Ceremonies: A Family View of Rites of Passage," in *The Family Life Cycle*, ed. Carter and McGoldrick, 429–60.

5. Steven J. Zeitlin, Amy J. Kotkin, and Holly Cutting Baker, *A Celebration of American Family Folklore* (New York: Pantheon Books, 1982).

6. Murray Bowen in the Preface to *The Family Life Cycle*, ed. Carter and McGoldrick.

CHAPTER 8

1. For those brave spirits who might want to explore further the complexities of this new epistemology, I would recommend Gregory Bateson, *Steps to an Ecology of Mind* (New York: Ballantine Books, 1972).

2. See P. Watzlawich, F. Weakland, and R. Fisch, *Change* (New York: W. W. Norton, 1974).

3. Two recent books relating family-systems theory and ministry focus primarily on family counseling: Charles William Stewart, *The Minister as Family Counselor* (Nashville: Abingdon Press, 1979), and J. C. Wynn, *Family Therapy in Pastoral Ministry* (New York and San Francisco: Harper & Row, 1982). William E. Hulme's *The Pastoral Care of Families* (Nashville: Abingdon Press, 1962) takes a developmental approach to the care of families but is not informed by the systems perspective as is Douglas Anderson's *New Approaches to Family Pastoral Care* (Philadelphia: Fortress Press, 1980).